NO GOD BUT GOD

a look at Hinduism, Buddhism, and Islam

by Del Byron Schneider

AUGSBURG PUBLISHING HOUSE
Minneapolis, Minnesota

NO GOD BUT GOD

A look at Hinduism, Buddhism and Islam

Copyright © 1969 Augsburg Publishing House

Library of Congress Catalog Card No. 74-84806

MANUFACTURED IN THE UNITED STATES OF AMERICA

Preface

This book is meant to stimulate rather than to satisfy completely the interest of readers today in the "big three" of the world's great Eastern religions, Hinduism, Buddhism, and Islam—Hinduism because it is basic to an understanding of Eastern thought, and Buddhism and Islam because today they, along with Christianity, are the great missionary religions.

I wish to acknowledge a literary debt to Huston Smith's *The Religions of Man* and John Noss's *Man's Religions*. For historical background, I know of no better book than that by Noss, who gives "the shape of the window" of the world's religions. The "view from the window" is portrayed by Huston Smith, who describes those elements in the religions which are alive and motivate men in the quest for faith.

I express my gratitude for the gracious help given to me by Swami Satprakashananda of St. Louis, Missouri. The fine selection of books in the library

v

of the Vedanta Society which he founded in St. Louis helped to emphasize the living and contemporary aspects of religion.

I wish to record, also, my appreciation to R. H. L. Slater, who retired in 1964 as professor of world religions and as director of the Center for the Study of World Religions, Harvard University, Cambridge, Massachusetts.

D. B. S.

Contents

CHAPTER ONE

Men
and
Their
Faiths

I will bring your offspring from the east, and from the west I will gather you; I will say to the north, Give up, and to the south, Do not withhold; bring my sons from afar and my daughters from the end of the earth, every one who is called by my name, whom I created for my glory, whom I formed and made. . . . Let all the nations gather together, and let the peoples assemble.

Isaiah 43:5-9

If there always had been but one culture or one language or one religion in the whole world, human beings probably would never have become aware of the nature of either culture or religion. But today man realizes, perhaps more profoundly than ever before, that he lives in a world of many cultures and many faiths. He uses such terms as East and West, even though he finds them difficult to define. He may know how he feels about the East, but he may have no precise idea what he means by the term. He knows that today no part of this planet is more than several hours away, and that no one can be indifferent to what happens anywhere in the world. He may tend to see people in terms of world

1

politics—and thus he may study other faiths simply to discover what is "wrong" with them, to set up standards for them which are not their own, or to uncover their weak points, rather than to understand them as they understand themselves. The general tendency in religion is that "people talk about other people's religions as they are, and about their own as it ought to be."[1]

How does one learn to understand and appreciate a people and a faith other than one's own? One approach is centered around three questions: How do the people make a living? How do they live together? How do they see themselves, other people, and the universe?

Agrarian or pre-industrial societies tend to be alike in their ways of making a living and establishing their social organizations, so that the distinctive differences among cultures generally can be traced to their different ways of seeing themselves and, from this perspective, of formulating their life ideals. For example, the missionary may proclaim to the Hindu the good news of a life after death, but this is not good news to the Hindu who all along has been seeking to escape one round of rebirth after another in life after death. The Hindu belief that religious truth is not absolute and that life is a series of rebirths in which progression is made in the understanding of truth strengthens his ability to live with many groups and to reconcile extremes in foreign policy, economic programs, and diverse religious systems. The way the Hindu understands himself and how he evaluates the goals of life thus puts a unique stamp on his culture.

---

[1] Wilfred C. Smith, *The Meaning and End of Religion* (New York: The New American Library, 1964), p. 48.

That India's way of seeing life is not, in many cases, that of the West's is pointed up clearly in the perennial problem of raising the nation's economic level to a standard Westerners think desirable. Under her five-year plans, India's economic progress barely keeps ahead of the population increase. A country, however, must want economic growth and seek it as an ideal; so before this happens in India there must be a change in attitudes, institutions, and traditions, because her cultural, social, and religious traditions do not place the same value on economic growth as those of the West.

Here we simply are faced with the fact that the Indian sees life differently than we do.

One of the ways, then, by which we can understand another culture is to ask: How do people think of themselves? As we study the philosophy, literature, art, and religion of Eastern people, we will find those elements that have shaped them, and religion is one of the doors we may enter for a fuller understanding of a people.

In discussing the place of Asian religions in the study of world history, Kenneth W. Morgan, the world religions expert of Colgate University, has pointed out:

> . . . religious faith—the ways men find meaning for their lives and evaluate their relations to the natural world, to each other, and to the transcendent —is a factor of basic importance in shaping a culture and influencing the process of history; that religion is not just one of many aspects of the history of a people, to be taken up when, and if, convenient, but is fundamental to historical understanding; that it is a necessary, but not sufficient, basis for the interpretation of history. A knowledge

of the religious background of the historical process under study will give meaning to much that would otherwise be obscure, will guard against possible misinterpretations, and might, even, lead to new perspectives on our own history and culture.[2]

"East" and "West"

One gain in the study of other men and their faiths is that the pictures in one's mind of other people are brought into truer alignment with reality. The tendency has been to deal with stereotyped notions about other people. Stereotypes sometimes are short-cuts to knowledge and can be useful, but too often they are rigid, commonplace assumptions that no longer conform to reality. We must be careful with such terms as "non-Western," "Asian," "Far Eastern," and "Oriental," for these terms also are generalizations. We constantly use the terms "East" and "West." What is the East and where does it begin? Where is the West and at what point does it end? We must define the terms "Eastern" and "Western." Labeling thought and culture as "Eastern" and "Western" is not at all scientific. There are great differences between the various beliefs and modes of conduct that have originated in the geographical East. F. S. C. Northrop emphasized in *The Meeting of East and West* that Eastern culture is so complex that we should speak of a *number* of cultures, as there are a *number* of countries with their own particular "civilizations." Northrop remarks, however,

[2] Kenneth Morgan, *Asian Religions.* An introduction to the study of Hinduism, Buddhism, Islam, Confucianism, and Taoism. A publication of the American Historical Association's Service Center for Teachers of History (New York: The Macmillan Company, 1964), p. 3.

that the factors which have distinguished one culture from another—separation by mountain ranges or vast expanses of land and water, differences of climate, varying forms of religion, naturalistic differences generating cultural diversities—also tie them together into a single civilization.

> Confucianism and Taoism are religions of Korea and of Japan as well as of China. Buddhism is as influential in China, Korea, and Japan as are Confucianism and Taoism. Buddhism and Hinduism occur in India, Ceylon, the Malay Peninsula, and the Southwest Pacific islands. Confucius, for all his originality, continuously insisted that he obtained his wisdom from a laborious study of the ancient classics. Lao-Tzu, the founder of Taoism, went back to the ancient classics also. Moreover . . . what he found there is precisely what the Buddha found in the ancient classics of the civilizations of India. Similarly, the founder of Buddhism claimed no originality, but insisted instead that he was returning a corrupted or overlaid Hinduism to its original source in the poetry of the early Upanishads and the even earlier Vedic hymns. . . . Thus, to specify the philosophical and religious differences entering into the constitution of the cultures of the East is at the same time to possess inescapable interconnections and identities. It is the unity provided by these essential relations and identities which merges the cultures of the Oriental countries into one traditional culture of the Far East.[3]

In our shrinking world, the distinctive features of the East and the West are vanishing and therefore one can appropriately speak only of the *traditional* ways of life in the East and the West, as Northrop

---

[3] New York: Collier Books, Collier-Macmillan, Ltd., 1946, pp. 312-313.

has done. We still are justified, however, in speaking of *Eastern* and *Western* religion, since the faiths themselves have retained their traditional aspects.

Broadly speaking, the religion of the East is made up of three major traditions: the Islamic tradition of Western Asia or the Middle East, the Indian tradition, and the Far Eastern tradition. In this book, the term Eastern has been limited to mean chiefly India, Southeast Asia, and East Asia. The broad geographic zone sweeping around the southern and eastern edges of Asia includes South Asia, Southeast Asia, and East Asia. South Asia is a new term, a substitute for the term "subcontinent," to denote India and Pakistan. Nine or ten independent states usually are regarded as part of Southeast Asia: Burma, Thailand, North Vietnam, South Vietnam, Cambodia, Laos, Singapore, Malaysia, the Philippines, and Indonesia. The word "Orient" is becoming obsolete. Some look upon China and Japan as the Orient. Others would include Korea and Southeast Asia. It is to be noted, however, that the word "Orient," used as the opposite of "Occident," does not necessarily carry a regional meaning and it has come to be applied to all of Asia.

A new term, East Asia, used to designate China, Korea, and Japan, now is preferred to "Far East," for "Far" implies that one is looking at the area from one's own perspective. This also is true of the term "non-Western," which sounds negative. In the case of Asia, we Americans often think as though we are still Europeans. Because we have inherited much of our directional outlook from Europe, we tend to regard any point in Asia as being East—"the East" being, of course, east of Europe. If we use the term "Far East," we use it in the way a Scandinavian or Italian uses it. In terms of distance such a viewpoint is not plausible. If in America we can overcome our antipodean way of thinking of the East, one of the great gains will be that, though we face one part of the East across the broadest ocean of all and the other part across an ocean and a great land mass, we will be aware that in the process of the cataclysmic shrinking of our world "the two ends [East and West] of its once flat surface have curled-up and come together." [4] The head-on convergence of races and cultures in a shrinking world and our meaningful encounter of this process will bring home to us the happy realization of what very close neighbors we really are. We will have gained immeasurably if we come to see the East as neighbor to our Western shores.

The Gain in Understanding

In our study of Eastern culture and religion, we may find that the traditional Eastern understanding of philosophy counterbalances Western philosophy and religion. For centuries, Western philosophy has been wedded to the physical sciences. Today we are beginning to see that science's critical approach to life may well destroy the West's religion and philosophy. Appreciation of the richness of Indian thought can be invaluable for the Christian, for the Judaic-Christian tradition came out of the same mold which has shaped so much of the Eastern way of thinking and doing. For the Christian it could mean a discovery of a dimension which was lost when the Greek —rather than the Hebrew—attitude of life had stamped European thinking to such a degree that

[4] Edwin O. Reischauer, *The United States and Japan* (New York: The Viking Press, 1965), p. 2.

even Christianity could not change the main direction of the European attitude of life.

It is usual in the West to separate the way of thought from the way of life so that philosophy becomes a kind of academic game that may or may not have anything to do with life itself. The Indian, on the other hand, seeks a practical orientation for his philosophy; he does not divide life into compartments such as religion, philosophy, and culture; for him the three constitute an integrated whole. He aims at translating into actual life what he thinks, knows, and believes. His way of life and way of thought have not become separated as in the West.

In *Philosophies of India,* Heinrich Zimmer, the scholarly Indologist, has compared this with what happened in the West.[5] Before Socrates, the Greek philosophers' approach to the mysteries of man and nature followed the logic of the natural sciences— mathematics, physics, and astronomy—that were becoming predominant. In the process, these philosophers destroyed their native tradition of mythology, which could not stand up under the logic of science. Zimmer reminds us, for example, that in the fifth century B.C. Anaxagoras was banished from Athens for declaring that the sun was not Helios, the sun deity, but a burning sphere. Socrates was accused of lack of faith in the gods and of undermining the belief of the young in the established religion. Thus the symbols of mythology disappeared or degenerated so that the gods' complicated love affairs and domestic quarrels became amusing themes for the poet and dramatist but never taken seriously. Establishing a close relationship with sciences gave Western philosophy an

---

[5] Joseph Campbell (ed.) (Cleveland: The World Publishing Co., 1956), pp. 27-34.

"increasingly secular, non-theological, practically anti-religious outlook on man and the world." [6]

Zimmer writes that in India mythology never ceased to be used as a vehicle of philosophic thought. Incarnations of the divinities and the traditions of the country's founding were used again and again by the *guru* or teacher. Such a close relationship between mythology and philosophy exists that Hindu culture is clearly embued with spiritual meaning, and philosophy draws upon the popular mythology which carries these truths and teachings to the masses.

Seeing Men as Men

The final great gain achieved through the study of another's culture is the ability to see men in the midst of historical and cultural differences. There are experiences common to all men as members of one human family, but in studying men and their faiths we must avoid two extremes: over-emphasis on the difference between West and East, so that the Easterner does not appear to be as naturally and reasonably human as we are, and the assumption that all people are like us. We can strike up this fine balance by being conscious of the fact that the same problems confront men everywhere, although solutions may differ. We also must constantly remind ourselves that one solution may not be any more right than another.

Differing ideas about marriage, for example, show how cultural conditioning shapes society's judgments. A child born into a family is dependent upon his parents for many years, for the family is the social insti-

---

[6] Heinrich Zimmer, *Philosophies of India* (Cleveland: The World Publishing Co.), p. 30.

tution whose main function is that of passing on culture. In Japanese culture, however, psychological dependence on the family becomes the basis of the rules of conduct between child and parent for life. Sano Chiye writes of the influence of the patriarchal family system with its authority and dominance as continuing for a lifetime:

> Social maturity in the traditional Japanese concept was attained by both sexes much later than physical maturity. . . . At a marriageable age a man or woman will still be socially immature, too inexperienced to be trusted with certain important decisions, including that of mate selection. Consequently, the responsibility of making arrangements for the marriage of young adults rested primarily with their parents and to a lesser degree with all the mature members in and around their families. Under ordinary circumstances, the greater part of this responsibility was discharged by the mother.
>
> The major motivation for parental arrangement of children's marriage was to protect the young individuals from the consequences of their possible faulty judgment. . . . The desires of the son or the daughter concerned were given due consideration as a condition of primary importance in the selection of possible candidates, and the final decision was usually left to the individual who was to marry.[7]

In the book *Marriage: East and West* by David and Vera Mace, the authors report an experience they had in India while discussing with a group of young people the idea of the Western type of "romance marriages." They had assumed that there

---

[7] Bernard S. Silberman (ed.), *Japanese Character and Culture* (Tucson: The University of Arizona Press, 1962), p. 113.

would be envy on the part of the young people who were "forced" to become partners in "arranged marriages."

"Wouldn't you like to be free to choose your own marriage partners, like the young people do in the West?"

"Oh no!" several voices replied in chorus.

Taken aback, we searched their faces.

"Why not?"

"For one thing," said one of them, "doesn't it put the girl in a very humiliating position?"

"Humiliating? In what way?"

"Well, doesn't it mean that she has to try to look pretty, and call attention to herself, and attract a boy, to be sure she'll get married?"

"Well, perhaps so."

"And if she doesn't want to do that, or if she feels it's undignified, wouldn't that mean she mightn't get a husband?"

"Yes, that's possible."

"So a girl who is shy and doesn't push herself forward might not be able to get married. Does that happen?"

"Sometimes it does."

"Well, surely that's humiliating. It makes getting married a sort of competition in which the girls are fighting each other for the boys. And it encourages a girl to pretend she's better than she really is. She can't relax and be herself. She has to make a good impression to get a boy, and then she has to go on making a good impression to get him to marry her."

Before we could think of an answer to this unexpected line of argument, another girl broke in.

"In our system, you see," she explained, "we girls don't have to worry at all. We know we'll get married. When we are old enough, our parents will find a suitable boy, and everything will be arranged.

We don't have to go into competition with each other."

"Besides," said a third girl, "how would we be able to judge the character of a boy we met and got friendly with? We are young and inexperienced. Our parents are older and wiser, and they aren't as easily deceived as we would be. I'd far rather have my parents choose for me. It's so important that the man I marry should be the right one. I could so easily make a mistake if I had to find him for myself." [8]

At Home in the World

Seeing man in his own historical and cultural surroundings in the East, we come away with a sharper appreciation of our Western culture. Those who are interested in the humanities, in religion, philosophy, art, literature, will find that the ancient cultures of India, China, Japan, and Southeast Asia are like mirrors that are held up to our own Western heritage. These ancient cultures show us our own distinctiveness and demonstrate alternative systems of value, belief, and action, different forms and expressions in fiction, poetry, and drama. The historian, economist, political scientist, anthropologist, and the sociologist whose interest lies in the social sciences will find the annals of human life and history in the East a source of richness that no longer can be ignored.

It is helpful to remember, also, that every civilization has had its golden eras. America is in the bloom of a great era at this moment in her history. In years past she has had to look to others for her existence, and she is still indebted to other cultures,

---

[8] David and Vera Mace, *Marriage: East and West* (copyright © 1959, 1960, David and Vera Mace), pp. 130 f. Used by permission of Doubleday & Co., Inc.

for her roots still lie in other civilizations. Islamic civilization had a great period in its history after the coming of the prophet Muhammad when it built not only a great empire, but a culture as well. Heirs of the ancient civilization that flourished on the banks of the Tigris and Euphrates Rivers, Islamic culture absorbed the main features of Greek-Roman culture and then acted as a medium for the transformation of feudal Europe into modern Europe. The Chinese look back with reverence and gratitude to their Golden Age of which their classics speak. The inventions of the Chinese—gunpowder, paper, and the compass—passed on to medieval Europe many of those influences which awakened the Western world to its renaissance. Today India is in debt to other cultures, but India has given as much as or more than she received. All of Southeast Asia's culture came for the most part from India, and all of East Asia is in debt to India for Buddhism, which helped mold the distinctive civilizations of China, Korea, Japan, and Tibet. India also has given the world such practical gifts as domestic fowl, sugar cane, rice, cotton, spices, the game of chess, and, perhaps most important of all, the decimal system. Greater than any of these, however, may have been the influence of ancient India's religious literature upon such men as Goethe, Schopenhauer, Fichte, Hegel, Emerson, Thoreau, and others.

All civilizations have contributed to the sum of human civilization. Western civilization, riding the crest of the wave today, is repaying a debt to other cultures. The day may come when the world will have a single culture, but until that day we must appreciate and gratefully learn from our differences.

CHAPTER TWO

Where
We
Are
Today

Behind all this general tendency for resurgence of religions in the plural, there is a quest for understanding the nature and significance of religion in the singular, or religion underlying religions. To that extent not only Asians but the people of the world everywhere in our generation are justified in talking about the resurgence of religion, as distinguished from religions. The prevailing mood of this Atomic Age in world history is to search for the meaning of faith. . . .

Paul Devanandan [1]

We begin our attempt in understanding by making an assessment of where we in the West stand in relation to the adherents of the religions of the East. We are told that as far as time and space are concerned "one world is in the making." Knowing that a little familiarity breeds confusion, we want to know our Asian neighbors better. Arnold Toynbee, the British historian, has reminded the West that while two or more civilizations have been in some touch with each other in the past, our own day for the first time sees these civilizations coming into intimate, vital, and dynamic contact with each other. We are becoming a neighborhood, but we are not as yet a brother-

[1] Quoted from his chapter "Renascent Religions and Religion," in *The Ecumenical Era in Church and Society*, Edward J. Jurji (ed.) (New York: The Macmillan Company, 1959), p. 150.

hood. How are people of different cultures and faiths going to live together? The fact that men worship in different ways is of tremendous significance, with economic and political as well as spiritual overtones.

The world learned once again just how significant these spiritual overtones are when in 1965 two neighboring powers, India and Pakistan, came to the brink of war over Kashmir. The struggle had been years in the making, and the basic issue was not politics or economics but religion. In 1947 Pakistan and India emerged as independent nations. An estimated half-million people were killed in Muslim-Hindu riots as panicky refugees fled toward the nearest friendly border. The point of contention still is unsolved today: to which country does Kashmir, with its 75 per cent Muslim majority belong—to Hindu India or to Muslim Pakistan, with its 120 million people?

According to Islam's mission-minded Ahmadiyya movement, there are 647 million Muslims around the world. Less partial statisticians lower the figure to a still impressive 465 million. Today 35 countries in Africa and Asia have Muslim majorities.

India represents Hinduism. Into a triangular wedge of the world only a third as big as the United States, India packs 480 million people, 360 million of them Hindus, and more than 200 million cows. India was the birthplace not only of Hinduism, but of Buddhism, which has spread from India throughout Southeast Asia into Japan and is steadily growing today.

Like Buddhism, Hinduism and Islam have experienced phenomenal growth in the last decades. Every year the crop of new babies in India exceeds the population of New York City. In much of West

Africa, Islam is said to gain converts at a nine-to-one
ratio over Christianity, and the end of this bur-
geoning growth is not in sight. Today the lands of
Asia and Africa contain more than two-thirds of the
world's population. In the next 20 years, according
to population experts, this part of the world will
have more people in it than there are in the entire
world today. The answers to the questions of how
to live together may have to be supplied by men
involved in the spiritual realm of life.

The World "Neighborhood"

One no longer can get by today with the traditional trite answers about another man's religion:
"My religion is true and all others are false," or
"All religions other than one's own can be ignored,"
or "All religions are the same, really." These will not
hold up today, especially if one has friends who are
members of other faiths.

How can a Christian continue to be a Christian
not merely in a Christian society or even in a secular
society, but in the world among Buddhists, Muslims,
and Hindus? The four great civilizations of our more
recent past were built around specific religions. In
India, China, the West, and in the Muslim world,
religious practices and not political beliefs or racial
origins were primary. If a Chinese, for example, did
not observe the laws of the family and the worship
of the ancestors and became a practicing Muslim,
he ceased being Chinese and passed over into the
Muslim civilization. If a Muslim became a Christian,
he not only changed his religion but his society.
Today this is rapidly changing. A Muslim must be
able to be a Muslim anywhere in the world; a Bud-

dhist must be able to carve a satisfactory place for himself in a world in which other men are Christians and Muslims. Since the East and West are being hurled at one another today with the speed of jets, the intellectual and spiritual barriers of even a decade ago no longer can stand. From the perspective of history, this dynamic meeting between East and West may be remembered as one of the most significant facts of this century.

The Christians of the West, for the first time, must seriously begin to understand people of other faiths. Christian believers never have had the world entirely to themselves, but for centuries they have acted as if a major portion of the world had been given to them exclusively. In fact, "Christendom" or Europe was only one of the major independent civilizations of the last thousand years, with China, India, and Islam as the other great world civilizations.

There has been almost no unity among these cultures, but today their independence and isolation is being broken down by a momentous revolution. Christopher Dawson, in *The Movement of World Revolution,* writes that when historians look back upon our years they may remember them not for the release of nuclear power nor the spread of communism but as the time in which all the people of the world first had to take one another seriously.[2]

The Search for Faith

Ours is a world where men are looking seriously for the first time at each other's faith, searching for the meaning of faith.

---

[2] Christopher Dawson, *The Movement of World Revolution* (New York: Sheed and Ward, 1959), p. 8.

The twentieth century has produced its own pro-
tests against scientific humanism and materialism.
The mood of ancient civilization has been character-
ized as anxiety brought on by the fear of death; the
mood of the Middle Ages as anxiety from condemnation and guilt, and that of the twentieth century as
"the anxiety of meaninglessness" and emptiness. This
has prompted the search for the significance of faith.
Nothingness, anxiety, meaninglessness, and despair—
these are the words used in our time to portray the
greatness of man in his "creative encounter with
nothingness and in his stoic courage of unyielding
despair."

Man's interest in the religions of others today has
to do with meanings and values. He realizes that religions do not speak only of rites and rituals and doctrines and gods. He wants to see how religion helps
men meet such problems as death, sorrow, tragedy,
isolation, and separation. He studies the faiths of
others to see in them men who are struggling to give
purpose and meaning to their daily lives.

Believers as Persons

As we examine other men's faiths, we see one another in terms of our common humanity. Today there
is a willingness to unmask the real issues and to lay
bare the real people. As we talk about a man's fears
and hopes, aspirations and loves, loneliness, agony,
and need, he not only becomes known but his beliefs are illumined. We often come to know one another through need. The loneliness of a teen-ager,
the heartbreak of a broken family, some inner defeat
or moral failure—life seems so constituted that within it are to be found the problems and needs that set

us thinking about religion and of help from one another.

The study of other religions ought to help men of the West discover the meaning of their own faith. For more than four centuries, the expansion of the Christian church coincided with the economic, political, and cultural expansion of Western Europe. But the people of Asia and Africa are now in revolt against this domination by the West. The religions of Africa and Asia are offering themselves as answers to the questions of mankind. Not since the first century A.D. have other religions thus seriously challenged Christianity.

During the second to the fourth centuries, the church fathers, Tertullian, the father of Latin theology; Origen, the best-known representative of Alexandrian theology (which aimed at a reconciliation of Christianity and Hellenistic thought); Justin Martyr, famous apologist and philosophical theologian; and Clement of Alexandria, teacher of Origen and leader of the Alexandria School, sought to relate Christian and pagan concepts and to defend the Christian's right to existence in a non-Christian society. From the eleventh to the fifteenth centuries the church was engaged in the Crusades, the "holy" wars against Islam. No one has yet suggested that the Christians learned anything from this encounter. It was not until the eighteenth and nineteenth centuries that Christianity "discovered" Hinduism, Buddhism, and the Chinese classics, and it is only within this century that we have realized that we must learn to live with one another.

In the course of history, Christianity has made at least three different approaches to the existence of other faiths. These have been described by Rajah

B. Manikam in *Christianity and the Asian Revolution* as an attitude of aggressive condemnation, of sympathetic appreciation and cooperation, and of proclaiming the uniqueness of the Christian Gospel, without denying the truths in other religions.

The West, however, may be able to learn something about religious coexistence from the East. Buddhists, Hindus, and Muslims have long known what it means to share their world with adherents of other faiths. One is not surprised to find Christian churches, Jewish synagogues, Hindu temples, Buddhist temples, and Muslim mosques in almost all of the large cities of the East. Within walking distance of the Imperial Palace in Tokyo there are several Shinto shrines, a Buddhist temple, a Jewish synagogue, two Christian churches, and the headquarters of one of Japan's so-called "new religions."

The meeting of the religions is not new in the Orient, nor is the aggressive condemnation of other religions. In his book *Crossing the Death Line,* Toyohiko Kagawa, Japan's great Christian leader, tells the story of his conversion and its effect upon his relationship with his uncle who was his guardian. After graduating from middle school, Kagawa felt led to study for the Christian ministry, and because of this decision he was compelled to leave his uncle's home. He was on his own, cut off from his family, and only with the help of foreign missionaries and his "beloved ragpickers" of the slums was he able to make a new life. The meeting of religions thus cuts across family life, social ties, and personal faith. As the Christian seeks to discover the meaning of religious coexistence, he will learn from the East involvement in something which is of deep concern to millions of human beings.

The Autobiographical Gospel

When Dr. S. Radhakrishnan spoke at the Center for the Study of World Religions at Harvard University in 1960, he remarked that Christians "should be stimulated by the resurgence of the non-Christian religions." Most of the criticism of the West is not directed towards the Christian people and their churches in the East, but against the West's Christian culture. The people of the East find it difficult to understand why Christianity is so lukewarm in the West, why it doesn't work more fervently for the "redemption of the West." They are dismayed that Christianity has failed to prevent the secularism of the Western part of the world. Prof. Slater writes: "Most of my Hindu and Buddhist friends expect me, as a Christian, to be missionary minded, in the proper sense of the term, as they themselves are missionary minded, and they have a right to question my Christian commitment and the value of any religious experience if I am not so minded. A fugitive faith is no whit better than a fugitive virtue and (to paraphrase a Buddhist saying) the greatest charity is the communication of our learning in the faith." [3] Resurgent Hindus, Buddhists, and Muslims do appreciate resurgent Christians. What they cannot appreciate is the Christian who is neither hot nor cold.

Kenneth Cragg, the Muslim scholar, has not permitted us to forget that, to men of other faiths, the Gospel is autobiography. The Christian is a personal dimension of the Gospel, the only dimension the Hindu, Muslim, and Buddhist see. The Christian, not his message, is the point of contact. Men must em-

---

[3] P. C. Jefferson (ed.), *The Church in the 60's* (Greenwich: The Seabury Press, 1962), p. 50.

body in what they *are* what God is doing in their lives. The Gospel, the words used to express it, and the life the Christian lives to manifest it must have content and reality, or they will say nothing. Missionaries returning from an overseas assignment often challenge American Christians to a renewal of faith, for they sense that many American church members are content "to be holding a religious faith that is of the consistency of a thin custard or a medium white sauce." The missionary knows that there have been enough travelers, tourists, and men and women stationed abroad, who, claiming to be Christian, could have made "mission boards obsolete" had their lives conformed to the profession of their faith.

Worldwide Vision

When we look at the world through the eyes of another people, the gains are enormous. We wonder at the Japanese mother with a baby strapped to her back clapping her hands together in worship before her Shinto shrine; the thinly clad Hindu stepping into the Ganges River for healing and cleansing; the Buddhist monk in his saffron robe begging for food at dawn on a main thoroughfare in Bangkok; the bewhiskered *meuzzin* crying aloud from the lofty and graceful minaret of the mosque, summoning the faithful to prayer; the dark-skinned boy wearing on his forehead the parallel marks of the god Vishnu as he receives the sacred thread from his priest as a token of assuming full religious duties; the thousands of faithful Muslims starting back at sunset to Mecca, accompanied by music, gunfire, and din in the final ceremony of the *hajj*; the shy behavior of yellow-robed Ceylonese monks carrying palmleaf umbrellas to hide their faces from passers-by as well as from the sun; the Hindu woman circling the sacred tree, reciting the scriptures and praying for the welfare of her baby; the Muslim who leaves his sandals at the door of the mosque to prostrate himself in prayer to the God of the prophet.

Our wonder leads us to welcome the encounter with men of other faiths. Every man exists in relation to God. We do not ask the Christian to hold his faith as anything less than it is—God's revelation in Jesus Christ. We do ask that as men worship and recognize the meaning of their existence in different ways, their experiences be taken seriously by the Christian, for religion is at work on things that matter the most. Death, sorrow, fulfillment, anxiety, meaning, value, purpose—these are the problems that confront men of all religions. And if we can learn from this "view from the top," our angle of vision will become broader and our faith will become larger.

Frank Laubach once wrote that as his heart was communing with God, "something broke within me, and I longed not only to lift my own will up and give it completely to God, but also to lift all the wills in the world up and offer them all in utter surrender to His will. To feel this great longing as I felt it then with all my being . . . is not this the highest longing one can ever feel?" [4]

---

[4] Frank Laubach, *Letters by a Modern Mystic* (Syracuse: Laubach Literacy Inc., 1955), p. 17.

CHAPTER THREE

Understanding Other Religions

We of the Occident are about to arrive at a crossroads that was reached by the thinkers of India some seven hundred years before Christ. This is the reason why we become both vexed and stimulated, uneasy yet interested, when confronted with the concepts and images of Oriental wisdom.[1]

We are being reminded frequently today that Western modes of thinking are not the most reliable tools for understanding the religions and cultures of Asia. The people of the East interpret life from their own perspective. Thus little understanding is gained by setting forth only doctrines, religious practices, and ceremonial observances. What is needed is a comparison of the faith of one religion with that of another. The historian of religions, Joseph Kitagawa of the University of Chicago, says that to understand we must enter as much as possible into the structure of Eastern thought and spiritual experience.

---

[1] Heinrich Zimmer, *Philosophies of India* (Cleveland: The World Publishing Company, 1951), p. 1.

The Western attitude toward reality might be summed up in the term coined from the Greek *philosophia*, meaning "a love of wisdom" based on reason. The Eastern attitude toward reality is best described by the term *"philo-ousia,"* from the Greek *ousia*, signifying essential being, and meaning "love of reality or essence." It is a love of experience which prefers intuition to reason.

In the West, subject and object are distinct; in the East, experience, intuitive knowledge, and the blurring of subject and object are important. The Westerner, therefore, has difficulty working himself into the world of his fellowman from the East. Eastern thought insists that there is a sphere beyond the realm of logical thought when one is dealing with the experience of reality.

"To express and communicate knowledge gained in moments of grammar-transcending insight, metaphors must be used, similes and allegories. These are then the very vehicles of the meaning, which could never have been attained, through the logical formulae of normal verbal thought," wrote Heinrich Zimmer in *Philosophies of India*.[2]

The East's civilization tends to develop the emotion; the West is objective and intellectual. The Eastern approach to life and reality is subjective and personal; it does not seek to reduce every human experience to the rational. The East, through men like Daisetz Suzuki, the interpreter of Zen for the West, keeps insisting that the key to the secret of being is not in the intellect. A Buddhist writer once said that the Buddha's teachings were like a raft which is left behind when the stream is crossed. One does not take the raft with him. Nor should anyone's

---

[2] *Ibid.*, p. 25.

concepts become so wedded to a teaching that they cannot be changed as experience dictates.

We in the West are beginning to understand this way of thinking. Some scientific concepts are seen today as a means for dealing with the world instead of understanding it. As such, we are prepared to accept the fact that each concept is useful and is to be discarded when it no longer works. This loosening of the West's attachment to concepts has opened the possibility for interpreting experience in many ways instead of in just one way which is taken to be *the* truth. Many people are beginning to feel that science or rational knowledge is not all-important. A certain distrust of rational knowledge which has appeared in the West should thus make it easier for us to understand the East.

Eastern "Reality"

The East insists that the West lacks spiritual perception. We may talk about faith and forget that talking about faith is not the same as experiencing it. Because religious experience in the East is nonverbal, a scholarly understanding of it is almost impossible. There is no alternative but to *practice* the religious experience and thereby to gain it.

This effort at grasping reality is one of Zen Buddhism's great attractions in the West. Zen's primary interest does not lie in understanding the world, but in helping the individual to an awareness of himself. Zen encourages a state of mind which is obsessed with this awareness of self and of life. Many are attracted to this state of mind in Western Zen which somewhat resembles the state of the mind of the East.

In a recent essay written after a visit to the East, Dr. Ernst Benz of Marburg, Germany, stressed the difficulties of understanding foreign religions.[3] His visit was embarrassing to him; he discovered that his academic knowledge of Eastern religions did not agree with the reality he had to face there. This experience on the part of a well-known scholar in the field of the history of religions led him to search for what made the understanding of Eastern religions so difficult for Westerners. He deplores the general trend in the West to study chiefly the historical aspects of Asian religions as they are recorded in their classical literature. It is obvious to him that the books and articles that come out of such studies are not reliable guides. Understanding of the reality of religious beliefs and practices in contemporary Asia can come only through empathy and a feeling of one's way in another man's religious experience, Dr. Benz writes.

The Nonpersonal God

We begin working ourselves into the religious universe of the Eastern mind by leaving behind our concept of God as a person. The Westerner of today is so imbued with the idea of God as a person, rather than a force or principle, that all his thinking is influenced by this. It is difficult to understand, therefore, that the personalistic idea of God is quite foreign to Hinduism and Buddhism.

To the Hindu, the idea of God is not built around a person but has more to do with infinite awareness, being, and joy. Sometimes this idea is represented

[3] See his essay, "Über die Schwierigkeit des Verstehens fremder Religionen," in *Geist und Werk, eine Festschrift* (Zürich: Rhein Verlag, 1958), pp. 245-266.

as a person because personality is one of the more intelligible and attractive concepts of which the human mind is capable, but Hinduism asserts that God is something above personality. When the sun cannot be looked at with the naked eye, a smoked glass is used, and the sun then is seen as a round disk. Similarly, when God in all his dimensions cannot be perceived as he is, we see him through our human spectacles; we understand only some aspect of him and thus think of him as a person. The heart of man yearns for a personal God of love, grace, and mercy. Eastern religions neither reject theism nor accept it as the last word in religious philosophy. The Hindu delights in the fact that his religion has achieved its great unity in diversity, by simply cherishing the many ways which men have represented and worshiped the various aspects of the Supreme Spirit.

The traditional Western reaction to this has been to label a religion without a personal God, especially Buddhism, as "atheistic." However, Buddha did not consider God personal because personality requires definition, which is precisely what Buddhism seeks to exclude. Since the experience of God or enlightenment cannot be transmitted by word or writings, Buddhism dismisses as unprofitable debates on the existence of God.

Creator and Creature

Another concept that needs modification is our distinction between the Creator and the creature. To the Western Christian the distinction between God and the world is a "must" of his faith. But among Hindus and Buddhists the idea of the oneness of all things and beings is basic to their thinking. Man possesses a double nature, a phenomenal self and a transcendental self. This transcendental self is the inner man, or the "spark of divinity" within the soul.

The rigid distinction in the West between the Creator and the created clashes with this concept of the "divine spark" thought of in the East as diffused throughout nature and mankind. The same divine reality that appears in the universe finds itself, according to Eastern thought, in the heart of man. This means that man may also be revered as divine. This accounts for the ease with which people in the East regard certain persons as embodying more of the divine than others, the classic example being that of the Japanese emperor. It accounts, also, for the ease with which they are able to worship many images as simple projections of a universe pervaded by the one Reality.

The Idea of Sin

Another basic Christian concept, the idea of sin, is held by the Easterner to be unworthy of any god. The word "sin" seldom is used anywhere in the East. Ignorance of one's true nature and of one's true relationship to the Supreme Spirit is the cause of man's misery in this life, Easterners believe. The idea of inherited sin is in conflict with almost everything an Easterner is brought up to believe. It undermines his very concept of existence. The human heart is not a reflection of evil, but of good.

Many people in the East believe that the doctrine of sin is a fantastic aberration of God whose wrath is unknown and whose goodness and serenity radiate over all. Such a doctrine, they believe, is wholly unfair to God, for it would make him a vengeful, peeking, bumbling sort who botched his job so badly that he was not able to keep evil out of his created world.

Functional, Not Theological

Another concept strange to Eastern religions is the idea that one can be a member of just one religious body. A Western Christian finds it odd that in Asia a person may participate in several religions without any sense of contradiction. In the Roman Empire during the early years of the Christian era, a Roman citizen could join several cults or religions without ceasing to participate in the rites of the state religion. Among the Chinese, Taoism, Confucianism, and Buddhism are mingled together, and in Japan people often are married in a Shinto shrine but are buried in a Buddhist ceremony. Buddhist temples and Shinto shrines ordinarily complement one another in their use. An average Japanese feels free to participate in the activities of both the shrine and the temple, depending upon the event he is celebrating.

To the Westerner it is incomprehensible that anyone should be affiliated with two or more distinctly different religions or even denominations. This is due to the strange occidental custom, the Easterner says, of regarding religion as a body of beliefs and practices which a member must accept to the exclusion of all other religions or denominations. Shrines and temples do not normally have members. Religion is geared to the functional, not the theological. Practices at any shrine or temple are meaningful and are accepted and enjoyed, regardless of their source.

There is little understanding in the East of the intolerance shown by Christianity. In fact, the Easterner wonders if the kingdom of God is so monotonous and so poor that it can manifest itself only in one single religion and one way of life. Thomas Ohm, the missionary author who has sought to acquaint European and American readers with what is thought about Western Christianity in Asia, points out that the individual can adhere to different religions at the same time because the East considers it a virtue in man to combine varied elements, especially religious elements that would appear to be contradictory.[4] The West likes clear distinctions; the East likes conciliation, compromise, and cooperation. The prevailing attitude of the East is that no religion can be true and perfect and express all there is to know about reality. All religions are variations of the same theme. Joka, the Zen master, penned these lines:

> *One moon, and one only,*
> *Is reflected in all waters.*
> *All moons in the water*
> *Are one with the one moon.*[5]

Doctrine's Role

This leads to the part doctrine plays in Eastern religion and why the Western concept of doctrine must be reexamined if we are to understand the Asian attitude. Doctrine is a characteristic of classical Christianity, so it is natural that in studying Asian religions we should be concerned with doctrine. But in the religious life of Eastern people, religion centers around liturgies, not doctrine or dogma. To be sure, sutras are recited and elaborate systems of doctrine are committed to paper, but these are seen as reli-

---

[4] Thomas Ohm, *Asia Looks at Western Christianity* (Freiburg: Herder, and London: Nelson, 1959).
[5] *Ibid.*, p. 32.

gious experiences, not truths. The reciting of sutras
is done to awaken a feeling that may lead to a religious experience.

Religion often becomes for the Westerner a concern of the mind, first, and of worship and action,
second. Thought and doctrine assume an important
role. In the East, the world of feeling and experience
and mood are primary. Nietzsche has said that the
real reason men hate the truth is because it is so precise. But men of the East say that in matters spiritual
it is better to be vaguely right than to be absolutely
wrong. Religious ideas simply cannot be precise.
Ideas and words should have vague and fluctuating
meaning which will help the worshiper form asso-
ciations of vast variety. To the Easterner the Western mind seems to make too much of a distinction
between subject and object, between that which
experiences and that which is experienced.

The East's fondness for grasping reality "with
naked hands" explains the scarcity of doctrinal for-
mulations in Eastern religions. Doctrines are too precise; important matters should be described only
vaguely. Zen teaches that the original content of
the Buddha's enlightenment never can be transmitted by words or writings. Many of the symbolic expressions used in the East, such as signs made with
the hands and fingers in Hindu dances and in Buddhist ceremonies, have great meaning for Easterners.
There is always the temptation to argue over a written doctrine while missing the religious experience
that lies beyond it. But religion is not something of
the mind. It is not enough to *know* of God and his
works; he must be *experienced* as close at hand.
Dogma *is* experience. The East prefers this kind of
truth, which it calls "experienced truth," to the kind

of truth which the West has come to call the "truths of faith."

Diversity, but Unity

Eastern religions find their greatest strength today in their diversity of religious expression while still holding to a basic unity. Buddhism, in fact, sees itself as the great "broker" between the religions of East and the West, between Christian, Muslim, and Hindu countries. There probably will never be mass conversions to Buddhism; such conversions, the Buddhist says, are not necessarily desirable. Intensified encounters seem certain, however, to produce some crossing over from one religion to another. Buddhism's hope is not to conquer its sister religions or to be absorbed by them, but, in the case of the Western religions, to effect a shift of emphasis. It hopes to strengthen the mystical, contemplative, and traditional elements, and turn the theistic religions more toward the awareness of the presence of God and less toward dogmatic assertions about the nature of God.

Hinduism harbors the same hope. Hinduism has tolerated all faiths and has, in fact, given birth to other religions. Hinduism asks the West to recognize that all religions are valid. Ramakrishna, India's great religious seer of the last century, summed up the Hindu position with words which have been quoted again and again to describe this vision of unity in diversity:

> Many are the names of God and infinite the forms that lead us to know Him. In whatsoever name or form you desire to call Him, in that very form and name you will see Him.
>
> In a potter's shop there are vessels of different

shapes and forms—pots, jars, dishes, plates, but all are made of one clay. So God is one, but is worshipped in different ages and climes under different names and aspects.

God is one, but many are His aspects. As one master of the house appears in various aspects, being father to one, brother to another and a husband to a third, so one God is described and called in various ways according to the particular aspect in which He appears to His particular worshipper.

As one can ascend to the top of a house by means of a ladder or a bamboo or a staircase or a rope, so diverse are the ways and means to approach God, and every religion in the world shows one of these ways.

Different creeds are but different paths to reach the Almighty. Various and different are the ways that lead to the temple of Mother Kali at Kalighat. Similarly, various are the ways that lead to the house of the Lord. Every religion is nothing, but one of such paths that lead to God.

As with one gold various ornaments are made, having different forms and names, so one and the same God is worshipped in different countries and ages under different forms and names. Though He may be worshipped in accordance with different conceptions and modes—some loving to call Him father, others mother, some calling Him friend, others calling Him the beloved, some praying to Him as the inmost treasure of their hearts, calling Him the sweet little child, yet it is one and the same God that is being worshipped in all these relations and modes.

As the young wife in a family shows her love and respect to her father-in-law, mother-in-law, and every other member of the family, and at the same time loves her husband more than these; similarly, being firm in thy devotion to the Deity of thine own choice, do not despise other Deities, but honor them all.

Bow down and worship where others kneel, for where so many have been paying the tribute of adoration the kind Lord must manifest Himself, for He is all mercy.

As the same fish is dressed into soup, curry, or cutlet, and each has his own choice dish of it, so the Lord of the Universe, though One, manifests Himself differently according to the different likings of His worshippers, and each one of these has his own view of God which he values the most.

As a toy fruit or a toy elephant reminds one of the real fruit and the living animal, so do the images worshipped remind one of God who is formless and eternal.[6]

[6] Swami Abhedananda (compiler), *The Sayings of Ramakrishna* (New York: The Vedanta Society, 1961), pp. 15-33.

CHAPTER FOUR

The Eternal Way of Hinduism

The One Reality, the learned
speak of in many ways.

Rig-Veda, I. 64 [1]

Sometime between 2000 and 1000 B.C. the inhabitants of India concluded that man lives in an impersonal world. In the twentieth century many in the West have come to the same conclusion and are finding in Indian thought not only a fascinating philosophy but fulfillment of their own religious beliefs. The religion of India has been described as a sort of philosophical algebra in terms of which all religious truths can be expressed.

On the twenty-fifth anniversary of the founding of the Vedanta Society in St. Louis, Missouri, Swami Satprakashananda reported that, in his years as mis-

---

[1] Kenneth W. Morgan (ed.), *The Religion of the Hindus* (New York: The Ronald Press, 1953), p. 50.

sionary to America, he never had sought to teach dogma or creed, for his religion is not an exclusive religion. He believes that his religion is the basis of all religions, for it embraces universal spiritual truths which underlie all doctrines. Hinduism, therefore, has universal appeal, for it is intended to make a Christian a better Christian, a Muslim a better Muslim, and a Hindu a better Hindu. Many Americans and Europeans have a genuine interest in this approach to religion. There is a likeableness about the religionist and his determination to coexist with anyone and everyone, whether he worships in a shrine, mosque, temple, church, or synagogue.

Hinduism's Appeal

Americans have been attracted to Hinduism in recent years because of Mahatma Gandhi, whose influence has extended far beyond the borders of his own country. Gandhi was a little man weighing less than a hundred pounds, but he was a sensitive man who represented the conscience of his nation and much of the world. For many people in the West he exemplified the spirit of the Sermon on the Mount. He himself acknowledged his debt to the teachings of Jesus and to the inspiration he drew from the Bible. One of his favorite sources of inspiration was the hymn "When I survey the wondrous cross." But when disappointments confronted him, he found his greatest comfort in the Hindu scriptures. "My life has been full of external tragedies," he said, "and if they have left no visible, no indelible scar on me, I owe it all to the teachings of the *Bhagavad-Gita*."

C. S. Lewis writes of his conversion that the only alternative to Christianity in his personal search for religion was Hinduism. He saw something of the greatness in Hinduism from which he felt he could profit. He had come to acknowledge God as one and as righteous. The question now was, "Where was the thing full grown? or where was the awaking? . . . There were really only two answers possible: either in Hinduism or Christianity. Everything else was a preparation for . . . these. Whatever you could find elsewhere you could find better in one of these!" [2]

Our concern in this chapter is to discover what in Hinduism commends itself to the West, motivates the life of Mahatma Gandhi, and captivates an intellectual like C. S. Lewis. Therefore we shall not touch upon the traditional Hindu goals and stations of life, the caste system still dominant in India, and the ashrams that are the source of much religious activity. Hinduism appears complicated enough as it is. India's religion has been the mainspring of her life and the mother of her culture. Her hills, mountains, rivers, lakes, seas, and cities have been made sacred by the touch of religion. Hinduism rests upon thousands of scriptural texts and includes within it a vast number of sects with their distinctive beliefs. Because India has been a land whose religion is infused with its folklore and mythology, its tradition and customs, it is extremely difficult to sort out what the Hindu really means by religion and what the essential elements of it are.

The Aim of Hinduism

While there is great diversity in Hinduism, the aim of all Hindu religion can be simply stated. Its goal is

[2] C. S. Lewis, *Surprised by Joy* (New York: Harcourt, Brace and Co., 1955), p. 235.

not merely to make man a perfect human being on earth or a happy citizen of heaven. In the words of Prof. D. S. Sarma of Vivekananda College in Madras, its goal also is "to make him one with ultimate Reality, the eternal, universal Spirit in which there are no distinctions—no cause and effect, no time and space, no good and evil, no pairs of opposites, and no categories of thought. This goal cannot be reached by merely improving human conduct or reforming human character; it can only be attained by transforming human consciousness." [3] Hindu literature is full of parables and metaphors, and the deities within the Hindu pantheon are numberless; all excite the imagination and open men's minds to the possibilities of oneness with Ultimate Reality.

Transmigration of Souls

One of the great affirmations that all Hindus make is that the transformation of human consciousness into divine consciousness cannot be done during a single life-span. It is not possible in one lifetime to make man's soul, called *Atman* by the Hindus, one with Reality, which the Hindus call *Brahman.* Hindu scriptures thus teach that the soul of man does not pass into hell, heaven, or purgatory, but is reborn into another existence which will end in due time and necessitate yet another birth. This repeated passing or transmigration of souls through this world is what is meant by *Samsara,* a word with great meaning in the Hindu lexicon; all of Hinduism takes its stand on this idea. Unlike Westerners, Hindus do not see time as a flowing river but as a pool of water. At intervals

---

[3] Kenneth W. Morgan, *op, cit.,* p. 3.

there are ripples in the pool, but the pool itself remains undisturbed. In the West we think of man's
life in terms of three score years and ten. In the East
we must take the long-range view of history, thinking
in terms of many lifetimes and thousands of years.

In the *Bhagavad-Gita,* one of Hinduism's best
known scriptures, Sri Krishna says to the warrior Arjuna: "You and I have lived many lives. I remember
them all: You do not remember." [4]

The fact is that birth inevitably is followed by
death and, Hindus believe, death by rebirth. And
the purpose? One is born again and again until the
soul *(Atman,* the true self which is enclosed in layers) becomes one with Reality *(Brahman).* It is in this
world that these layers are stripped off and the stages
of perfection worked out. So long as he does not attain oneness with the Divine Being, man continues
to go through repeated births. In the grand cosmo-
logical scheme the individual bits of life, of which
man is the highest form, are reborn again and again,
passing from vegetables to animals, from animals to
human beings, from one human body to another,
until they are pure enough to return to *Brahman,*
their spiritual source.

Karma and Mukti

What determines the nature of man's next birth,
what causes his soul to enter a higher or lower state
of existence, is the law of *karma,* which means that
one's thoughts, words, and deeds fix one's lot in future existences. The law of *karma* implies that every-

[4] Christopher Isherwood, and Swami Prabhavananda (trans.).
Bhagavad-Gita (New York: A Mentor Book, 1954), IV, p. 50.

The Shiva is the great Hindu dancer who dances in the sheer, playful joy of creation.
Shiva is not only a god who destroys but one who creates, and the rhythm of
Shiva's dance is that of a world perpetually forming and dissolving and reforming.
The postures which the Indian artists give to this aspect of Shiva are some of the
most beautiful in Indian art.

The serene figure of Amida Buddha is the altar symbol in the sanctuary of the Matava Buddhist Temple in Saginaw, Michigan. Amida Buddha is the Japanese name for the Buddha of the Pure Realm or Land. Rebirth in the Pure Realm is attained by faith in the power of Amida's vow to save all beings and by the calling of the Buddha's name in faith.

This head of a Japanese figure is variously identified as an image of Sakyamuni (the historical Buddha) or of Maitreya (the Buddha of the Future or the Buddhist Messiah). This figure is in wood, in Koryu-ji, Kyoto.

LOCATIONS OF THE FOLLOWING RELIGIONS:

HINDUISM

BUDDHISM

ISLAM

CHRISTIANITY

Christ in the *yoga* posture as the Hindus see him. Some Easterners believe that Christ may have spent his time in this fashion in the 40-day wilderness experience.

(JESUS CHRIST IN HIS YOGA POSTURE.)
"HE WAS THERE IN THE WILDERNESS...
AND WAS WITH THE WILD BEASTS."

A *yogi* in the *yoga* position known as the Lotus Posture, one of the meditative postures conducive to prolonged contemplation.

In the middle of the city of Mecca is the open-air building known as the Sacred Mosque. In the center of the courtyard is the darkly shrouded Kaabe, one of the holiest shrines in Islam and the center or focus for the yearly pilgrimage.

An Eastern impression of the figure of the classical Christ. The emphasis is on the flat, meditative features with its downward contemplative position of the eyes.

thing a man does determines destiny. This process is quite impersonal. There is no judge, no punishment, no repentance, only the law of cause and effect. A man reaps what he sows; his deeds shape his character and his soul. Man is the builder of his future, and it lies within his power to determine what that future will be. If a man has devoted all his energies to the pleasures of life, he cannot hope to be reborn into a higher world. The soul-awakening point in a man's life, therefore, comes when, playing one round after another of life's game and winning them all, he "comes to himself" and wishes that life had something more to offer.

Since before the time of Christ the mind of India has been at work on this question. The answer of Hinduism is, as Huston Smith reminds us: Yes! Life does hold something better! No matter how much a man has of this world's goods, he is not satisfied because what he really wants lies on a deeper level. He wants more of *Being* itself. He wants to be *fully* alive to the universe and to the self within him. Man wants these things in unlimited or infinite degree. One of his most distinctive features is that he can grasp the idea of infinity. This capacity colors his life. Life gives him glimpses of joy, knowledge, power, but in his true self *(Atman)* he has these without measure, since the self is essentially one with God. Mention any good and man always can wish for more of it. Man wants infinite being, infinite knowledge, infinite joy, but his highest aspiration is for *mukti*—release from the wheel of rebirth and from the power of *karma*—and for freedom from the limitations that imprison him within his present existence.

Four Ways to *Brahman-Atman*

Hindus believe that infinite being, awareness, and joy not only are within man's reach but are his already. A man is not just a body and a personality; underlying that personality and giving it life "is a reservoir of being that never dies . . . " and is without limit in awareness and joy. This hidden center of his life is *Atman*. *Brahman* is the objective All; *Atman* is the subjective Self. Ultimate Reality is, therefore, *Brahman-Atman*, a term acknowledging the objective and the subjective as one.

But how does a man discover the true self? How does he find God? Through centuries of religious practice, Hinduism has discovered four basic paths that lead to union with God. These paths are for men of different temperaments and natures. Some people want action, others prefer contemplation; some are emotional, others are rational and philosophical. The paths, called *yogas* (one who practices *yoga* is a *yogi*), lead men to an awareness of their oneness with Ultimate Reality. Hinduism says the oneness has been there all along but by *yoga* (i.e., yoking of the mind to God) men become joyfully conscious of that fact.[5]

Psychological Exercise

Some people will not take anything on faith; they have to be shown. For these people Hinduism prescribes the way of *raja-yoga* or physical and mental exercises for psychological discipline. Dogmas, beliefs, and rituals are not prescribed; there is nothing to "believe in." This pathway is simply a graded

[5] Swami Nirvedananda, *Hinduism at a Glance* (Vidyamandira, Bengal: S. Mandal, 1946), pp. 63-106.

course of mental concentration. The goal of liberation or *mukti* is reached when the mind becomes absolutely still and absorbed in *Brahman*. To achieve this, the mind must be helped to concentrate. Through special postures, methods of breathing, and rhythmical repetition of the proper thought formulae, man breaks through all the layers—body, personality, and individual consciousness. The *yogi* is able to say, in effect, "I am smaller than the smallest atom, likewise greater than the greatest. I am the whole of the great multicolored-lovely-strange universe. I am from the beginning. I am Man and I am the Lord; I am God himself." The purpose of this discipline is to demonstrate that man is a layered being, and that he must drive into the deepest part of his being to find his true self.

Swami Nirvedananda of the Ramakrishna Mission in Calcutta outlines the eight successive courses prescribed in *raja-yoga* through which the devotee must pass before his mind is opened to the infinite. The first two courses are meant to cleanse the personality, to create self-control, temperance, continence, truthfulness—moral qualifications one must have before one sees God. The next step is to train the body to sit erect, with the spinal column held rigid and the head, neck and chest held in a straight line. This is practiced until one is able to sit motionless for at least an hour. Rhythmic breathing also helps concentration. The denial of the body is important, for no further advance can be made until the body is under complete control.

The next step is the "drawing in of the sense organs." The eyes, ears, and other organs of the body are only outer instruments; attached to them are the inner organs. For example, when the eye sees a flower, the inner instrument of sight produces the flower image in the mind. Thus it is also with color, sound, smell, taste, and touch—each sensation acts upon the mind, and the mind acts upon the will. I see a flower; my mind tells me to pick the flower. In other words, thoughts agitate the mind, and unless the inner organs are detached from the outer instruments, the mind will never reach the calm needed for the apprehension of Ultimate Reality.

The *yogi* is prepared next to attack the subconscious mind. This is done by letting the mind run on and on and simply observing the thoughts that come up from within the depths of the mind. This is known as "emptying the mind." As the mind gradually empties, the thoughts become slower and the mind becomes steadier. The powers of observation, memory, and will-power increase as the restlessness of the mind decreases. When the mind has reached this stage, it is ready to concentrate on a single object. We have seen pictures of Hindus sitting along the banks of the Ganges in the yogi position concentrating on their navels or other parts of their anatomy. Swami Nirvedananda says there is a purpose for concentrating on one object, for as the mind appears to flow in an unbroken stream toward the object, the mind loses its grip on all other things and reaches the final step called *samadhi,* meaning the condition of the mind which is completely absorbed in God.

As in a deep sleep a man becomes unconscious of everything about him, in the state of final absorption, or *samadhi,* even the object of meditation disappears as the power of controlling the object is gained. Now the final stage is reached; the mind becomes perfectly still. When this happens, the last of the layers sheathing the mind have been removed and the self stands revealed in its true relationship. The individual has come to realize that the very core of his being is nothing but God. He has reached the goal. There is nothing for him to long for or to desire; he has been transformed.

Oneness Through Knowledge

The second pathway is called the way of knowledge *(jnana-yoga)*. This is a difficult path most often walked by the philosopher. Its results are the same as the others; it leads to union with God and to a state of bliss. The search is for the real self *(Atman)*. Hinduism says that man, however, does not know his true self and that this is the cause of human misery and evil.

What is man's chief ignorance? His inability to distinguish between the real (God) and the unreal (the material or the universe). Man persists in thinking himself a real and separate being when this is not the case at all. The objective-subjective All or *Brahman-Atman* is the only real being, but as long as man continues the illusion of separate selfhood, he is bound to "the wheel, eternally revolving."

Hundreds of analogies have been used to clarify and illustrate the centuries-old truth in Hinduism that man does not have a separate selfhood. The *Upanishads* suggest the following:

> The individual is also said to be like a wave rising from and sinking again in the sea, or like a drop of spray, which momentarily flies above the sea. . . . A drop of brine held apart from the ocean, flying, let us say, across the face of the sea, may be viewed under two aspects; under the first, it appears to be an individual drop of a certain size

and consistency, with a particular location in time and space differentiating it from any other drop or any other entity whatever; under the second view, however, this is a misleading description of the case, for the drop is in reality *only the ocean in the air,* it is after all only *apparently* a thing by itself, a pure individual.[6]

Through analogies such as this the Hindu understands that all the surface appearances which common sense accepts as being exactly as they seem are in reality a part of *Brahman-Atman* and not at all what they seem.

How does man break through this illusion and ignorance? The first step, according to Swami Nirvedananda, consists in hearing the truth about the real self. Only a sage or teacher *(guru)* can speak with illumination on the subject, and he must be approached with humility and expectancy so that he will disclose the secrets of self-knowledge. The second step is some good, hard thinking. Observation and study may help us learn much about the universe; however, we know very little about *ourselves.*

When I say, "This is a horse," I surely mean that the horse is something distinct from me as an object of my experience. I don't confuse the horse with myself. The same holds true when I say "my body" or "my mind." I mean that the body and mind are distinct objects of my experience, and yet the Hindu emphasizes that we *always make them the subject.* This covers up our real nature and shows us as something that we are not. Hinduism says that the same soul is present in every creature, from the smallest amoeba to the most liberated sage. The difference

[6] John B. Noss, *Man's Religions* (New York: The Macmillan Company, 1956), pp. 230-231.

between them is only in degree. In our ignorance we think the body is the all of reality. But as we advance in knowledge we come to understand that the body is only the casing.

During sleep we do not perceive anything or perform any kind of action, yet we do not cease to exist. When we wake up, we say we have slept soundly. On whose evidence? The active part of our being was not on stage; yet there remained something in us that witnessed the sleeping, something that never goes to sleep. It exists always. And this, Swami Nirvedananda says, is our real self, the constant *witness* of all actions and experiences. This "witness" is the soul; this is the objective All or Ultimate Reality, *Brahman,* in whom all things have their being. Thus day by day we are to live our lives thinking of ourselves in the third person, all the while meditating as profoundly as possible on our identity with the universal Spirit. Like so many moons, men's souls shine with the light of the same Sun. When a man has thus taken the universe layer-by-layer and has reached its core, he comes to that moment of realization which leads to union with God.

Oneness Through Love

The third way to realize oneness with the eternal spirit is *bhakti-yoga,* or the way of love and devotion. This way rests on the simple truth that one can realize God by loving him. Nothing else is expected—no great exercises of body and mind. The second of the pathways, the way of knowledge, is said to be the shortest path to supreme realization, but this course is too difficult for most people; they continue to be religious in their own way, and the way of love has become for them the most popular. This has given rise in India to many different sects centering on salvation through devotion. There is no denial of the ways of mental discipline, knowledge, or work, but the majority steadfastly claim that devotion to God is the true way of salvation.

Most people are emotional by nature. Love is the one emotion that influences and sways us more than any other emotion. We love ourselves, our families, our relatives, our country, our homes. Our love for these determines our activities and shapes our conduct. Our fear of death arises from our love of life. Hatred springs from excessive love of self. Indeed, noble as well as evil deeds owe their origins to this ruling emotion. Selfless love is the prime mover of all that is good; excessive self-love is the inspiration for all that is evil. Love is like the lamp that may be made to illumine an altar as well as to set a house on fire; it depends on how it is used.

Hindu scriptures are full of instances of the transformation of self-love to the love of God. Huston Smith relates the story of one famous sixteenth century mystical poet of India, Tulsidas, who was excessively fond of his wife. He could not bear to be separated from her for even one day. One day she visited her father's house, but Tulsidas followed her and met her there. At that his wife remarked, "How passionately attached you are to me! If you could shift this attachment to God, you would realize him in no time." This remark shocked Tulsidas so that he became "a passionate lover of God," who helped others find him.

The way of love (*Bhakti-yoga*) suggests that the goal of life (*mukti*) can be reached if we love God with the same intensity with which we love something on earth. We all know how to love another person; we are required only to shift the focus to God. But loving God is not as easy as it seems to be. To love an object that pleases our senses is one thing, but to love God whom we neither see nor feel is quite different. Hinduism's way of love and devotion, which Christianity and Islam consider the only pathway to God, includes a graded course through which a novice may gradually develop. Hinduism believes the present life is only one in a series of lives and that men are in different stages of their journey. Thus it prescribes the kind of discipline which will suit a man's condition and will help him pass on to the next plane.

> If the metaphysical ideal is too advanced and abstract for man, a theological ideal is set before him. At this stage the impersonal Absolute, *Brahman*, becomes a personal God, the perfect becomes the good, manifestation becomes creation, liberation becomes life in heaven, and love takes the place of knowledge. If he is not even fit for this stage, a course of ritualistic and moral action is prescribed for him. At this level the personal God is represented by an image in a temple, ritual and prayer take the place of meditation, and righteous conduct takes the place of love.[7]

Hinduism's several hundred images of God, its myths, and its magnificent symbols point the devotee to what lies beyond the symbols. Though God is formless, he appears through myriads of forms. It is wise, Hinduism teaches, for the worshiper to attach himself to some deity that has manifested itself. The best ideal for most persons is one of God's human

---

[7] Morgan, *op. cit.*, pp. 4, 5.

incarnations. This is the worship of God in the form
of what Prof. Sarma calls "one's chosen ideal." The
idea that God has projected the universe out of himself makes it easier for the worshiper to think of him.
The idea of God's presence in nature also can be in-
stilled with the help of Hindu mythology. Its stories,
parables, and legends may be with or without historical basis; some are allegorical, some are full of poetic
imagery, some are narrations of events of the legen-
dary past. Through them all the abstract and highly
subtle ideas of Hinduism are conveyed to the mind
of the common man. As he learns to worship his
"chosen ideal" and as he practices his devotion
day by day, he has the promise of Krishna: "Those
whose minds are fixed on me in steadfast love, wor-
shiping me with absolute faith, I consider them to
have the greater understanding of *yoga*." [8]

Enlightenment Through Works

This leads to the fourth and final way which is
the way of works, or *karma-yoga*. As we have seen, it
is not the only way. Like Ramakrishna, the great
nineteenth century Indian saint known as the "living
synthesis of all religions," a man may choose to devote his life to the worship of God; or he may, like
Sankara, the exponent of the Advaita (monism) system of philosophy, seek to realize God through
philosophical inquiry; or he may choose, like Mahatma Gandhi, to lead an active life in the world and
make every one of his actions an offering to God. The
way of works is the way for the active man, without
giving up home or his duties, and yet proceeding

[8] *Bhagavad-Gita, op. cit.*, XII, p. 97.

straight to the goal of perfection. This is the method-
ical way of carrying out rites, ceremonies, and duties
that add to one's merits or favorable *karma*. Hinduism says that you do not have to retire to a cloister
to realize God; you can find him in the world of
everyday affairs as readily as anywhere else. It is the
attitude that counts and not the nature of the work
that is done. There is a way of living in the world
that makes for the highest spiritual achievement,
and this is the way of *karma-yoga*.

Man must learn the secret of work that turns every
secular duty into worship. We sometimes think of
Mahatma Gandhi as a political leader with deep religious commitment. The Hindu sees him as a religious
leader with deep political convictions, for his political activities were mere by-products of his intense
religious faith and experience. How is this possible?
Yoga is defined as "sameness of mind" that surrounds
the self under all circumstances. Duty for duty's
sake is the formula. While one is doing his work, one
does not wish to see the results of the work. Work
done in this manner leads to complete detachment,
almost disassociation from self. Profit or loss, triumph or defeat, whatever the result, it will be received with equal grace. The whole point is to
transcend the smallest of the finite self. Every deed
that is done for the self puts another grain in the
wall that prevents the self from breaking through to
the infinite. Every good deed selflessly done takes
away another grain, and the soul is that much closer
to realizing its potentiality.

But how can contemplation and prayer and calm-
ness of mind be preserved when one remains actively
engaged in the hustle and bustle of the day's work?
It depends on the viewpoint. As we have seen, the

real or *Brahman* alone exists. We, however, live under the illusion that thousands of objects constitute this universe; we even believe that we are real and distinct subjects of action. This does not conform to reality; this is really *maya*. *Maya* is not simply "illusion," because the universe is real in a sense. Those myriads of objects are illusions insofar as they do not appear to be what they really are, a part of *Brahman*.

The true self of man does not act or experience, nor does it undergo any change. Realizing this, it is possible for a man to be extremely active and yet completely self-possessed, for it is not work that disturbs the calm of the individual, but his desire to see the results of his work. If he could be detached from his work, if he could stop the longing to behold the fruits of his action, no amount of activity would ruffle the calm of his mind. Normally it is the desire for the fruit that leads us to sow the seeds of action. Now, if we give up the desire for the fruit, will we lapse into inertia? No. *Karma-yoga* prescribes detailed attention to one's duties without, however, any desire at all to see the outcome.

To illustrate the almost complete detachment one must cultivate, a story is told of the *yogi* who sat meditating on the banks of the river Ganges. A scorpion fell into the water beside him. He scooped it out, only to have it bite him. The scorpion fell in again. Once more the *yogi* reached down to rescue him and once more he was bitten. Twice more the sequence was repeated. A bystander who had been watching this incredible incident asked the *yogi*, "Why do you keep rescuing the scorpion when its only gratitude is to bite you?" "It is the nature of scorpions to bite," was the reply. "It is the nature of *yogis* to help others when they can." [9] The way that leads to enlightenment is work performed in this spirit without thought of the consequences. The *yogi* who has achieved this state feels he has become the unmoved and changeless "witness" of all that goes on in his body and mind. "All work done without attachment; all action surrendered to God" is his song.

Samadhi—the Goal

These, then, are Hinduism's four pathways that lead to union with God. The goal of each of the ways is to bring man to understand the true reality that underlies all the appearances of reality and help him to reach that final goal of union with the Infinite called *samadhi*—the state in which man's mind is completely absorbed in God. This is the religious quest in Hinduism; this is the "pearl of great price."

By means of the four *yogas*, which are intended to suit the temperaments of all men but are not exclusive of one another, the religious believer has attained what he sought—personal proof of the existence of *Brahman* and his identity with it. He has reached the final insight; he has said: "Truly, that thou art." For centuries Hinduism has been calling man to seek after God "as a miser pants after gold." For thousands of years for the religiously-minded in India the main spiritual quest has been to rise above the cycle of rebirths, to achieve union with the Absolute. Today Hinduism calls all men everywhere to a ceaseless search *in their own way* for the Eternal One. "Truth is One"; it is men who call it by different names. It is

---

[9] Huston Smith, *The Religions of Man* (New York: A Mentor Book, 1959), p. 31.

this vision of unity in diversity that has commended
itself to different people of different lands. Hinduism
today is again showing signs of its original dynamism.
Its future is hardly in doubt. The words of Mahatma
Gandhi "with their paradoxical and typically Indian
identification of true progress and return to the start-
ing-point may well be the words of Mother India
herself:

"Consider my spinning wheel. A full turn of the
wheel is called a revolution. . . .
"Those who want to mock me and my spinning
wheel say, 'You want to put the clock back.'
"No, my friends, I am the most advanced revolu-
tionary, and I need only let the clock go on for it
to come back to the starting point of its own
accord.
"A revolution is a return to the First Principle,
to the Eternal. Some cling to the forms of the past
and the memory of the dead, and they live like the
dead; others hurl themselves into foolish novelties
until they plunge into the void. I go forward without losing my way, for I am always coming back
to the most ancient traditions through a complete
revolution, a total but natural reversal, willed by
God and coming at its appointed time." [10]

---

[10] R. C. Zaehner, *The Concise Encyclopedia of Living Faiths* (New
York: Hawthorn Books, Inc., 1959), p. 260.

CHAPTER FIVE

The
Way
of
the
Buddha

There is only one whom we might be inclined to compare with Jesus: Buddha. This man is a great mystery. He lived in an awful, almost superhuman freedom. Yet his kindness was powerful as a cosmic force. Perhaps Buddha will be the last religious genius to be explained by Christianity. As yet no one has really uncovered his Christian significance.[1]

Buddhism, unlike Hinduism, owes its origin to a founder. Siddhartha is the given name and Gautama the family name of a man who is judged by hundreds of millions of people, from Ceylon to Japan, and throughout large sections of the Asian mainland, to have exerted, by his intellectual integrity, moral persuasiveness, and spiritual insight, the most pervasive influence on the thought and life of the human race.

Pious Buddhists reverently avoid his personal name; they refer to him as *Sakya Muni,* a teacher of

[1] R. Guardini in George Appleton, *On the Eightfold Path* (New York: Oxford University Press, 1961), p. 23.

the Sakyas, for he was born of a minor noble of the Sakya clan. They call him *Tathagata*, or Truth-revealer, but the name by which he is commonly known is Buddha. The term "Buddha" is not a proper name but an honorary title which means "Enlightened One" or "I Am Awake." It is a title like Christ or Messiah, except that it is not limited to one individual.

"The Buddha" is a confusing term as a description of the founder because there are many Buddhas; anyone who achieves complete enlightenment becomes a Buddha. But the one which millions revere in the East and who is known in the West simply as "Buddha" is Siddhartha Gautama who was born in what is now Nepal near the border of India around 560 b.c. He lived for 80 years, and his life, like that of other founders of religion, has become a profound example to millions of his fellowmen.

Gautama's Early Years

Little really is known about Gautama's birth and childhood. His biography has become interwoven with a great mass of Oriental legend with which for centuries Asians have lovingly surrounded it. Stories of wonders such as a miraculous birth, simultaneous conversion of thousands of disciples, previous and future incarnations, and volumes of alleged teachings written centuries after his death make up this story. There is little doubt among scholars, however, that Gautama was a historical person and that the picture of the world in which he moved and the teachings which he advocated can be learned with reasonable accuracy. It is interesting from the comparative point of view to look at the legend that has grown up around Gautama.

It is said that on the fifth day after his birth Hindu astrological experts were called by his father to forecast his future. It was foretold that two careers were open to him, that he would become either a "universal monarch" or the "Buddha Supreme" of the world. Tradition insists that his father wanted his son to become a world-wide ruler, and therefore decided that he should be brought up in the royal tradition. Above all, he should be spared from seeing what has come to be known as the famous legend of "The Four Passing Sights." The soothsayers had predicted that if the child witnessed these four sights, the four signs of what life really is—old age, sickness, death, and a wandering ascetic—he would forever renounce his life of royal pomp and turn his back on the life of a universal monarch for that of a homeless monk.

When Gautama was 16 he was married to a beautiful princess who bore him a son called Rahula. Legend declares that Yasodhara, his wife, was "majestic as a queen of heaven, constant ever, cheerful night and day, full of dignity and exceeding grace." Gautama and his wife lived in luxury; their robes were "made of the finest fabrics from Benares"; day and night a white umbrella was held over them so they would not be troubled "by the cold or heat or straws or dust or dew." Three palaces were built for them, "one for the rains, one for the winter, and one for the summer," and his father had them fitted "with every kind of gratification for the five senses." But it became apparent that this bliss was not to last for long, and it was evident that Gautama was destined to become more and more a stranger in his father's household.

The Four Passing Sights

At 29 years of age Gautama experienced "The Four Passing Sights." According to the story of Gautama's early life, his father had him attended always by young companions. Whenever his son left the palace, his pathway was cleared of all but youths and maidens so that he was kept ignorant of the common fate of men. The tradition is that Gautama also would have grown up ignorant of the other, less attractive companions of life—old age, disease, and death—had not the gods themselves intervened to assume the shapes that would awaken the young prince to his destiny. One day Gautama asked his charioteer to make ready the state carriage and drive to the park.

Now the young lord saw, as he was driving to the park, an aged man as bent as a roof gable, decrepit, leaning on a staff, tottering as he walked, afflicted and long past his prime. And seeing him, Gautama said: "That man, good charioteer, what has he done that his hair is not like that of other men nor his body?"

"He is what is called an aged man, my lord."

"But why is he called aged?"

"He is called aged, my lord, because he has not much longer to live."

"But then, good charioteer, am I, too, subject to old age, one who has not got past old age?"

"You, my lord, and we, too, we all are of a kind to grow old, we have not got past old age."

"Why then, good charioteer, enough of the park for today. Drive me back hence to my rooms."

"Yea, my lord," answered the charioteer, and drove him back. And he, going to his rooms, sat brooding, sorrowful and depressed, thinking, "Shame, then, verily be upon this thing called birth, since to one born old age shows itself like that!" [2]

On another day the young prince saw the second sight, that of a desperately sick man who had fallen by the wayside and was being lifted and dressed by his friends. For the first time Gautama knew how physical misery attends man all the days of his life. The young prince came upon the third sight, according to legend, when he saw a great group of people constructing a funeral pyre for "the corpse of him who had ended his days." This time the prince learned that all men are subject to death, that no one has passed beyond its reach. These three sights robbed him of his peace of mind. His father tried to cheer him up with elaborate entertainment in the form of dancing girls, for he said: "We must not have Gautama declining to rule; we must not have him going forth from the house to the homeless state; we must not let what the Brahman soothsayers spoke of him come true."

Although his father increased the pleasures and the abundance that surrounded him, Gautama became more and more distraught. His vision of life had changed; he knew now what life really was, and with it came an insatiable hunger to escape from the kind of living to which he was subjected in his father's home. It was the fourth of the "Passing Sights" that showed Gautama the way out of his predicament. As

---

[2] E. H. Brewster, *The Life of Gotama The Buddha*. Compiled from the Pali Canon (London: Kegan Paul, Trench, Trubner and Co., Ltd., 1926), p. 15. For the early years of the Buddha, I also used Henry C. Warren's *Buddhism in Translation* (Cambridge: Harvard University Press, 1896), pp. 1-110. Also Paul Carus, *The Gospel of Buddha* (Chicago: The Open Court Publishing Co., 1915), pp. 1-259.

he and his charioteer were driving in the park, a shaven-headed man, a recluse, wearing the yellow robes of a monk, appeared before him. Here was a calm ascetic whose appearance gave witness to the fact that he had found the answers to the riddle of life. Gautama asked him:

> "You, master, what have you done that your head is not as other men's heads, nor your clothes as those of other men?"
>
> "I, my lord, am one who has gone forth."
>
> "What, master, does that mean?"
>
> "It means, my lord, being thorough in the religious life, thorough in the peaceful life, thorough in good actions, thorough in meritorious conduct, thorough in harmlessness, thorough in kindness to all creatures."
>
> "Excellently indeed, master, are you said to have gone forth, since so thorough is your conduct in all those respects." [3]

The words of the monk were balm to the young prince's restless heart. He was resolved to leave his father's home to seek that peace of mind and to gain that freedom from old age, disease, and death that he now knew pressed upon all human existence.

The Buddhist scriptures describe in loving detail the lonely struggle of the young prince in deciding to renounce his high place in the world. His father commanded more and more girls "skilled in all manner of dance and song, and beautiful as celestial nymphs" to satisfy every whim of the brooding prince. But his father was fighting a losing battle. The young prince's increasing aversion to passion did not allow him to take pleasure in these spectacles. One

---

[3] Brewster, *op. cit.*, p. 18

night, after a whirl of lavish entertainment, the prince fell into a brief slumber.

"And the women exclaiming, 'He for whose sake we should perform has fallen asleep. Of what use is it to weary ourselves any longer?' threw their various instruments on the ground and lay down. And the lamps fed with sweet-smelling oil continued to burn."

The scriptures, as translated from the *Majjhina Nikaya*, the second "basket" in the Pali Canon, tell how the prince then rose and, stepping with inner revulsion over the sprawling forms of the sleeping women, left forever the room which had become "like a cemetery filled with dead bodies impaled and left to rot." [4] He made his way to his wife's chamber, and there, gazing fondly down on the sleeping mother and his infant son, he bade an unspoken farewell. That night he shaved off his hair and beard, exchanged his rich garments for the coarse yellow robe of a monk, and walked into the forest to become part of that great anonymous group of monks vowed to live the religious life.

The Wandering Seeker

Gautama was obsessed with the idea of religion—which lies so close to the mind of every Indian—and was willing to face the rigorous discipline necessary for gaining the religious end. He left the land of his native Sakyas and went to Rajagaha, the capital of the neighboring kingdom of Magadha which extended along the Ganges valley. He wandered from place to place in search of a teacher who would guide him to his goal. He first became the disciple of two Hindu

⁴John B. Noss, *Man's Religions* (New York: The Macmillan Company, 1956), pp. 156-158.

masters who were trained in *raja yoga,* and who in-
structed him in their own doctrine and discipline.
But he did not find their techniques compatible to
his nature, and he became convinced that the substance of Hinduism or Brahmanism would not conduct him to true enlightenment. There was another
way open to him; this was the extreme bodily asceticism which some were then advocating.

He began a series of fasts, engaged in exhaustive
exercises of meditation, and inflicted on himself aus-
terities of the worst kind. He came to realize that as
"fire cannot be produced from damp but from dry
wood only," those whose passions are not calmed cannot attain enlightenment. If it was his body that was
holding him back, he was determined not to allow
one sinew to stand in the way. He abandoned food
and became a mere skeleton. According to the rec-
ords of his life, "with gritted teeth and tongue cleav-
ing to my palate I mastered, crushed, and forced my
thought by the mind until the sweat oozed out from
under my armpits." He sat on a bed of thorns, dressed
in a hairshirt and other irritating garments, and let
the dirt accumulate on his body until it dropped off
of its own accord. He reduced his diet to "one or two
beans a day" and became exceedingly thin. The rec-
ords say:

> Like dried cane now became my arms and legs,
> withered by this extremely scanty diet; like the
> foot of a camel became my buttock; like a string
> of beads became my spinal column, with the verte-
> brae protruding through; just as the roofbeams of
> an old house sharply protrude, so protruded my
> ribs; just as in a deep well the little water-stars far
> beneath are scarcely seen, so now in my eye-balls
> the sunken pupils are scarcely seen; as a wild

gourd, freshly cut, in the hot sun becomes empty
and withered, so now became empty and withered
the skin of my head. . . . And when I wished to
touch my belly, I reached the back of my spine,
and when I wished to touch my spine, I again
reached to the belly.[5]

Gautama's Enlightenment

Mortification of the flesh and severe asceticism did
not lead Gautama to the spiritual insights he desired.
Though he often found himself at death's door, he
was no closer to the riddle of life than when he first
started. "Six years of search along the two most
widely recognized roads to salvation known to India,
philosophic meditation and bodily asceticism, had
yielded no results." [6] Finally, having decided that
asceticism was not the way to enlightenment, the
record of his early life shows that he remembered
how once in his youth, "sitting under the shade of a
rose-apple tree, aloof from desire, aloof from things
not good," he had an experience of mystic contemplation. He wondered now whether this might not be
the path which would lead him to the highest wisdom.

Thus it was that in his 35th year on a full-moon
evening in May he seated himself at the foot of a
tree, which has since come to be known as the *bodhi*
tree (meaning "enlightenment"), situated near Gaya
in northeast India. Here he entered upon a process of
contemplation and meditation that brought him to
the climax of his inner struggle. Having seated himself firmly, cross-legged, he made a solemn and his-

[5] Brewster, *op. cit.*, pp. 35, 36.
[6] Noss, *op. cit.*, p. 161.

torical resolution that was to lead to his enlightenment and to a change of thinking in the lives of millions of people. According to the *Majjhima Nikaya,*
he resolved: "Let my skin and sinews and bones become dry . . . and let all the flesh and blood in my
body dry up, but never from this seat will I stir, until I have attained the supreme and absolute wisdom."

At this point tradition has recorded a great temptation scene. Mara, the Evil One, "the bringer of
death and the enemy of truth," realizing that Gautama was about to pass beyond his control, rushed
his evil forces to the *bodhi* tree to disrupt his concen-
trations. The Tempter, with his three daughters,
Tanha, Raga, and Arati, and his host of evil demons
sought to kindle desire in the heart of the Buddha-
to-be. In one of the temptations, the Tempter dis-
guised himself as Death. The personification of evil
and his powerful hosts assailed the aspirant with
great thunderstorms, showers of rocks, and live coals
that came smoking and flaming and crashing through
the air, followed, finally, by a great darkness. But
because of the strength of his perfections from previous births, Gautama remained unmoved; the flames
of hell became wholesome breezes of perfume, and
the angry thunderbolts were changed into lotus
blossoms.

In one final, desperate act the Evil One challenged
Gautama's right to be doing what he was doing, to
be piercing, as it were, the very secrets of the universe. Thereupon, drawing forth his right hand from
beneath his robes, the Buddha-to-be stretched it out
toward the mighty earth and said, "Are you witness,
or are you not . . . ?" And the mighty earth thun-
dered, "I bear you witness!" with a hundred, a thou-

sand, a hundred thousand roars, as if to overwhelm the army of Mara. While Mara's army was put to flight, the host of the gods descended from heaven and made offerings of garlands, perfumes, and ointments, and in many a hymn extolled the victor. While the *bodhi* tree, in homage, rained "red coral-like sprigs upon his priestly robes" that fateful night in May, and while Gautama's mind was at last piercing the bubble of the universe, the record says that the earth quaked 12 times, lotuses bloomed on every tree, fruit trees were weighted down by their burden of fruit, and the whole earth became like a bouquet of flowers while the oceans became sweet to the taste and the rivers checked their flowing. For 49 days he stayed under the *bodhi* tree, deep in rapture, after which his "glorious glance" opened again onto the world with its remedy for the ills of mankind. With this triumph a new chapter opened in the history of man's spiritual achievement.

However, the Buddha was confronted with a temptation far more insidious than the direct assaults of the Tempter. The scriptures state that he was besought by the Evil One to keep this newly-won truth to himself. After all, who could be expected to understand such truth? Men would misunderstand him, for they would not be able to comprehend "what goes against the stream, abstruse, deep, difficult to perceive, and subtle." Would it not be better to keep to himself what he obtained through so much effort? Why not simply enter the blessed state of the hereafter or *Nirvana* and be done with the world forever? In one of the best-attested facts in the record of the Buddha's life,[7] we are told

---

[7] See T. W. Rhys Davids, *Buddhism: Its History and Literature* (New York: G. P. Putnam's Sons, 3rd edition), pp. 104-105.

that this temptation was real to him—the temptation
to pass away without attempting to proclaim to others the glad tidings of the noble way. But after intense mental struggle he began his preaching ministry declaring that "there will be some that will understand the *dharma* (the truth)."

The Buddha adopted a mendicant missionary's life
with its poverty, unpopularity, and opposition. He
did not merely preach, but he lived the kind of life
which he taught other men to live. He is reported to
have preached his first sermon in the Deer Park in
Benares in northern India. He urged his disciples to
avoid the two extremes of sensual pleasure and self-
mortification and to follow the middle course. In-
spired by his preaching, thousands came forward to
become resident members of the Buddhist monastic
order called the *Sangha.* The rules for admittance
into the order were few: the wearing of the yellow
robe, the adoption of the shaven head, the carrying
of the begging bowl, and the habit of daily meditation. Every initiate subscribed to the confession: "I
take refuge in the Buddha, I take refuge in the
Teaching *(Dharma).* I take refuge in the Order
(Sangha)."

Here was a threefold vow symbolizing the Buddhist trinity—not a triune deity but a faith with three
aspects. From the very beginning monks were en-
couraged by Buddha to undertake the work of missions, for in the words which have now become famous Buddha said: "Go forth, mendicant brothers,
upon journeys for the help of the many, for the well-
being of the many, out of compassion for the world
. . . for the well-being of spirits and men." [8]

---

[8] Joseph Kitagawa, *Religions of the East* (Philadelphia: The Westminster Press, 1960), p. 160.

For a while Buddhism became the dominant religion of India and, under King Asoka in the third century B.C., trained missionaries were sent out to spread the teaching in all directions. This continued until the subsequent eclipse of Buddhism in India and the development of Theravada Buddhism in southern Asia.

For 45 years the Buddha himself traveled far and wide, and the number of his disciples increased with each passing year. "Brahmins and monks, hermits and outcasts, noble ladies and repentant sinners" joined the community. About 480 B.C., when the Buddha was 80 years old and on one of his preaching trips, he journeyed to an obscure town by the name of Kusinara, northeast of Benares. Before leaving on the slow three-month journey, he had predicted to Ananda, his cousin and favorite disciple, that his time had come to enter *Nirvana,* that place where his earthly existence would come to an end. According to the traditional story of his life, while dining one day at the home of Cunda, a goldsmith, he came down with severe dysentery, evidently caused by some poisoned food. Despite his critical condition, he continued toward Kusinara, but when he could journey no more, he lay down under the shady bough of a tree. His last words to his disciples were:

> *"My age is now full ripe, my life draws to its close:*
> *I leave you, I depart, relying on myself alone!*
> *Be earnest then, O brethren, holy, full of thought!*
> *Be steadfast in resolve! Keep watch o'er your own*
>   *hearts!*
> *Who wearies not, but holds fast to his truth and*
>   *law,*

*Shall cross this sea of life, shall make an end of
grief."* [9]

The Path Is the Goal

While there is little in the legend of the Buddha's
early life that can be set down with confidence as
sober fact, it is clear that here was a man who combined in rare degree a gentleness, serenity, and compassion that aroused in his followers a devotion such
as only the greatest leaders of men have awakened.
Many Westerners who have come to know Buddhism's yellow-robed monks and have investigated
the vast libraries of their centuries-old monasteries
consider Buddhism "one of the noblest edifices of
thought ever created by the human spirit." And yet
Buddha himself was not interested in constructing a
system of thought or in purely philosophical speculation. His concern was with the meaninglessness of
human life, the pain and futilities of his fellowman,
and the way of escape from them.

He rejected philosophical speculation *(jnana yoga)*
as the way of salvation, for he said that the solution
to the mysteries of life does not depend on human
thought. Man does not gain insight into the meaning
of existence and the way of deliverance simply
through knowledge. Buddha also rejected all special
revelation and appeals to authority or tradition and
every outward ceremony and system of sacrifices. He
rejected religious devotion *(bhakti yoga)* as a way of
salvation, believing that the universe abounded in
gods and demons and superhuman powers, but these
were all finite and not in control of man's destinies.

---

[9] E. A. Burtt, *The Teachings of the Compassionate Buddha* (New
York: The New American Library, 1955), p. 50.

What preoccupied Buddha was not a theory about the world, but the path leading to the salvation of fellow human beings from the wheel of birth and rebirth. If a man thinks at all, he should devote his thinking to controlling his desires and not in constructing elaborate doctrinal statements, Buddha believed.

"The important thing in Buddhism," says de la Vallee Poussin, "is not dogma, but practice, not the goal, the mysterious and unascertainable Nirvana (of Hindu background), but the Path." [10] Though his system later incorporated elements of elaborate metaphysics, Buddha held that man's difficulty was not so much "in the way he philosophizes," but "in the way he feels." As we shall see, Buddha declared that doctrines were useful and necessary only in helping people understand the nature of life's transitoriness and the importance of moral discipline and spiritual insight.

Thus this was the dialogue between Buddha and one of the monks who came to him full of wisdom and pious dialectical subtleties:

"Reverend Sir, it happened to me, as I was just now in seclusion and plunged in meditation, that a consideration presented itself to my mind, as follows: These theories which the Blessed One has left unexplained, has set aside and rejected—that the world is eternal, that the world is not eternal . . . that the saint neither exists nor does not exist after death—these the Blessed One does not explain to me. And the fact that the Blessed One does not explain them to me does not please me nor suit me. I will draw near to the Blessed One and inquire of him concerning this matter. . . . "

---

[10] Kitagawa, *op. cit.*, p. 162.

And Buddha replied with the parable of the arrow smeared with poison:

"Did I ever say to you, 'Come, Malunkyaputta, lead the religious life under me, and I will explain to you either that the world is eternal, or that the world is not eternal . . . or that the saint neither exists nor does not exist after death'? . . . Anyone who should say, 'I will not lead the religious life under the Blessed One until the Blessed One shall explain to me (all these things)' . . . that person would die before the Tathagata had ever explained this to him. . . . It is as if, Malunkyaputta, a man had been wounded by an arrow thickly smeared with poison, and his friends and companions, his relatives and kinsfolk, were to procure for him a physician or surgeon; and the sick man were to say, 'I will not have this arrow taken out until I have learnt whether the man who wounded me belonged to the warrior caste, or the Brahmin caste, or to the agricultural caste, or to the menial caste.'

"Or again he were to say, 'I will not have this arrow taken out until I have learnt whether the man who wounded me was tall, or short, or of the middle height.'

"Or again he were to say, 'I will not have this arrow taken out until I have learnt whether the man who wounded me was black, or dusky, or of yellow skin.'

"That man would die, Malunkyaputta, without ever having learnt this.

"The religious life, Malunkyaputta, does not depend on the dogma that the world is eternal; nor does the religious life depend on the dogma that the world is not eternal. . . .

" . . . There still remain birth, old age, death, sorrow, lamentation, misery, grief, and despair, for the extinction of which in the present life I am prescribing. . . .

"And what have I explained? Misery, have I explained; the origin of misery, the cessation of misery; and the path leading to the cessation of misery have I explained. And why have I explained this? Because this does have profit, has to do with the fundamentals of religion, and tends to aversion, absence of passion, cessation, quiescence, knowledge, supreme wisdom, and Nirvana; therefore have I explained it. Accordingly, Malunkyaputta, bear always in mind what it is that I have not explained, and what it is that I have explained." [11]

The question that presented itself to Buddha as the question that needed an answer, above all, was the question of life itself. There is not a map lying around on the face of life that can point men to a more coherent and meaningful life. In what way ought one to live so as to come into a satisfying relationship with the mysterious universe and attain the fullness of joy of liberation? In what way can life with its pain and suffering be reset so that it is again in joint? The answers which Buddha offers to these personal questions are unmistakably clear. He held four profound convictions about life known as "The Four Noble Truths." We may anticipate their significance by outlining them in the following way:

I. At the core of life is misery, pain, suffering.

II. This unhappiness is caused by selfish desire, craving for finite existence.

III. Selfish craving can be destroyed.

IV. It can be destroyed by following "The Noble Eightfold Path," whose steps are:

[11] Burtt, *op. cit.*, pp. 33-36.

1. Right understanding
2. Right aspiration
3. Right speech
4. Right conduct
5. Right livelihood
6. Right effort
7. Right mindfulness
8. Right absorption

The Truths and the Path

I. "Now this, monks, is the noble truth of pain;
birth is painful, old age is painful, sickness is painful, death is painful, sorrow, lamentation, dejection,
and despair are painful. Contact with unpleasant
things is painful, not getting what one wishes is
painful." [12]

Birth and death, suffering and love, are universal
facts of human experience. Buddhism teaches that
they are also the signs of a lack of inner harmony or
state of discord in the universe. Suffering, or *dukkha,*
means more than just physical pain; it is the pain of
heart and mind. Conflict is at the very root of man's
existence.

"The Buddha's first Truth is one that was recognized by William James when, applying the scientific
method to the study of *The Varieties of Religious
Experience,* he formulated his first conclusion in the
words 'there is something wrong about us as we naturally stand.' " [13] The impermanence in everything
that appears to exist, the ceaseless change, the end-
less becoming that is never quite satisfied or com-
pleted, some escape from it can and must be found,
Buddhism says.

---

[12] *Ibid.,* p. 30. See also Burtt's translation for Truths II, III, IV.
[13] George Appleton, *op. cit.,* pp. 52, 53.

At the core of life, Buddha felt, was misery. Buddhists believe that the truth of this conviction is evident today in the way men try to distract themselves with worldly pleasures and ephemeral pursuits. Gabriel Marcel writes:

> Do you not sometimes get the impression that we are living—if it can be called living—in a broken world? Yes, I mean broken, just in the sense in which a watch can be broken. The spring is no longer working. As far as outward appearances go, nothing is changed. Everything is in its right place. But if you put the watch to your ear, there is nothing to be heard. You understand; this world— what we call this world, the world of men—at one time or another it must have had a heart—but now you get the impression that this heart is no longer beating.[14]

Albert Schweitzer understood the human situation as Buddha experienced it when he said:

> Only at quite rare moments have I felt really glad to be alive. I could not but feel with a symphony full of regret all the pain that I saw around me, not only that of men, but of the whole creation.[15]

Dukkha really means an "axle which is off-center" or a "bone which has become dislocated." Something has gone out of life, something has gone wrong with it. Buddha recited some occasions when the dislocations of life bore down particularly heavily upon men as, for example, in the experience of birth and old age, in the trauma of sickness, death, and dejection. Human life is steeped in pain, misery, and suf-

---

[14] Stephen Neill, *Christian Faith and Other Faiths* (New York: Oxford University Press, 1961), p. 187.
[15] Huston Smith, *op. cit.*, p. 108.

fering, and all of life, Buddha believed, is out of joint; it is not what it appears to be on the surface. Until the gap between the real and the impermanent is bridged, until the estrangement is overcome, no lasting happiness will come to man.

II. "Now this, monks, is the noble truth of the cause of pain: the craving, which tends to rebirth, combined with pleasure and lust, finding pleasure here and there; namely, the craving for passion, the craving for existence, the craving for non-existence."

If men can detect and eliminate the cause of suffering, suffering itself will disappear, Buddhism says. Here the Buddha has identified the cause of life's dislocation as *tanha,* usually translated as "desire" or "craving." In the use of this word, however, we must observe that in spite of what many Westerners have come to believe, Buddha did not advocate the extinction of all desire. Indeed, there were some desires that he passionately advocated, such as the desire for release from rebirth. Buddha taught that all existence is impermanent and without substance. Whatever exists is in a state of constant flux. It is due to man's ignorance, rooted in desire and attachment, that *things* are thought to have substance. *Tanha* then becomes a specific desire for those things which are not real because they have no entity.

In Buddha's scheme, even rebirth takes place without any actual substance passing from one existence to another. This is expressed in the word *anatta.* Instead of the Hindu belief that an imperishable and substantial soul *(Atman)* goes over from one life to another, Buddha's reflection upon his soul led him to deny that any of its elements had permanency.

What men call life, he taught, is really only an impermanent aggregation of constantly changing states of being or *skandas,* among which are the body, feelings, conceptual knowledge, instincts, and consciousness. As long as these are held together, the individual functions as a single being, lives, and has a history. When the self dies, no finite self as such dies and is born again; there is only continuity of causes and conditions. All that passes over to the next life is the *karma*-laden consequences of one life causally determining another. Where does the flame of a candle go when it is extinguished? In the same way go the *skandas* of men.

But as man sees himself, he thinks of the world and of himself as having permanent substance. The things of the world look lasting to him, and he thus strives for their possession and clings to them. In reality they are fleeting phenomena, and since they have no stability at all, they cannot be of solace to him. The true nature of things, then, says the venerable Balangoda Ananda Maitreya of Ceylon is this: All existence is impermanent *(anicca)* without substance *(anatta),* and this brings only suffering *(dukkha),* because man desires *(tanha)* those very things that can only bring despair and disappointment.[16]

III. "Now this, monks, is the noble truth of the cessation of pain: the cessation without a remainder of craving, the abandonment, forsaking, release, nonattachment."

The third Truth is a simple prescription for cure: "destroy, stop, abandon, relinquish, and reject the root cause," that is, *tanha,* or desire. But how is the

---

[16] Kenneth W. Morgan (ed.), *The Path of the Buddha* (New York: The Ronald Press, 1956), p. 81.

root cause to be dug out? This is not a process that can be achieved quickly. Man must be made over by long and patient discipline. A totally different person must come into being, a person cured of life's crippling disabilities. Buddhism does not speak of codes and laws and rites, but of training and rigorous practice designed to release the individual from a life ruled by impulse, ignorance, and desire. To accomplish this, Buddha called for a program of action. He prescribed a treatment for life as it really is and not what men imagine it to be. Buddha broke his program of action down to eight steps. The way to reset life, to overcome the estrangement from reality, is to follow the technique of the Middle Way described in the Noble Eightfold Path.

IV. "Now this, monks, is the noble truth of the way that leads to the cessation of pain: this is the Noble Eightfold Way; namely, right views, right intention, right speech, right action, right livelihood, right effort, right mindfulness, right concentration."

The way of the Buddha represents an eight-rung ladder of perfection. George Appleton, who has given us a sensitive and sympathetic approach to Buddhism in *On the Eightfold Path,* says that the word "right" used here is of the same root as the Latin *summum,* meaning the highest or best. The Eightfold Path is more than a code of morality; it is a way of life. The first two steps of the path are simply an awakening, a summons to abandon the old way by which truth and destiny are missed. This involves an act of will and of heart. The man who achieves greatness is usually compelled by one consuming aspiration or idea. He may do many things throughout the day, seemingly without reference to his consuming passion. Behind all he does, dominating and influencing his life, must be the one thing that counts supremely.

The next group of three steps, known as the ethical disciplines, are based on the assumption that he who has taken up the life of holiness must avoid the extremes of "eat, drink, and be merry" and the ascetic extreme of self-mortification. The last three steps of the Eightfold Path—right effort, right mindfulness, right absorption—constitute a course of mental discipline and training that leads straight to *Nirvana* or the end of becoming. We are the result of what we have thought, the Buddha said in effect.

The remarkable thing about man is that he often deceives himself. His thoughts and feelings follow a pattern which keeps him from seeing himself as he really is until through intense self-examination the props upon which he has rested give way to the realization that existence really is impermanent. This understanding alone, however, is not sufficient, for while a man may understand reality, he may not realize it. The supreme realization occurs when the mind and the senses are no longer active, when through absorption all thought ceases. Joy runs deep in this realization, for the individual has a foretaste of the future. For the rest of his days he will know release from misery-bringing desires. He awaits with contentment and without apprehension the "putting out of his lamp of life"—the entrance into *Nirvana* at death.

The End of Life—*Nirvana*

Just what *Nirvana*, or the final state of man, will be, Buddha did not explain. The word means "blown out," "become cool," or "extinct." It might appear that with nothing "passing over," since the soul or self is unreal *(anatta)* and thus without substance, *Nirvana* is annihilation. Buddha did not say that. He did not know whether that was true or not. All he cared to know was that *Nirvana* was the final peace, the eternal state of being. His disciples had seen in the Buddha a reality which they wanted in their own lives. Their testimony is that progress along the path which Buddha advocated brings an enlargement to human life as well as the hope of eternal bliss.[17] But how to describe for his followers the state in which all identification with a man's historical, finite self is obliterated while experience itself remains and is magnified beyond all imagination, did not occupy the mind of the Buddha. The path itself, not the goal, was the important consideration. When he was asked by a wandering monk if it was possible to illustrate by a simile the place called *Nirvana*, the Buddha replied:

> "If a fire were blazing in front of you, would you know that it was?"
> "Yes, good Gotama."
> "And would you know if it were to be put out?"
> "Yes, good Gotama."
> "And on its being put out, would you know the direction the fire had gone to from here—east, west, north, south?"
> "This question does not apply, good Gotama."

The Buddha then closed the discussion by pointing out that the question the ascetic had asked about existence after death was not rightly put, either. "Feelings, perceptions, those impulses, that consciousness" by which one defines a human being have

---

[17] Morgan, *op. cit.*, pp. 111-112.

passed away from him who has attained *Nirvana*. "He is deep, immeasurable, unfathomable, as is the great ocean." [18]

Theravada and Mahayana Buddhism

The two branches of doctrine that have grown up around Buddha's teaching are Theravada Buddhism, whose followers generally are the southern Asians in Ceylon, Burma, Laos, Cambodia, and Thailand, and the Mahayana Buddhism of China, Japan, and Tibet. From early times the type of Buddhism practiced in China, Japan, and Tibet differed from that of the south Asian Buddhists. The difference is traced back to about 200 years after Gautama's death, when a group of his disciples disagreed on the interpretation of his teaching and preached a way of life which was less rigorous and more easily adapted to the needs of the common man. This doctrine became known as *Maha-yana*, the "big raft" or the "greater vehicle," and its members referred to orthodox southern Buddhism as *Hina-yana*, "the little raft" or the "lesser vehicle." The southern Buddhists, however, prefer the name *Theravada*, the Way of the Elders, implying a claim to represent Buddhism as taught by Gautama himself. Mahayana Buddhism spread in the north, and its tenets differed so greatly from those of Buddhists in the south that they constituted almost a different religion.

Mahayana Buddhism found the monkish life of the south too severe and demanding for the common people. It sought a way of making Buddhism a religion of the masses, a method by which enlightenment

---

[18] Burtt, *op. cit.*, 115-116.

might be achieved more simply. Where the ideal
Buddhist of the Theravada groups remained the holy
man who attained enlightenment for himself alone,
the ideal Buddhist of the Mahayana became a saintly
figure known as a *Bodhisattva*, a holy person who had
vowed not to enter *Nirvana* until the whole human
race had achieved salvation. Thus in the north, "salvation by faith in the *Bodhisattva*" became one of
Buddhism's basic tenets. Since early times the *Bodhisattvas* have formed a great company of supernatural beings who hear prayers and come actively to
men's aid.

The prevalent view of *Bodhisattvas*, especially in
China and Japan, is that they are beings who made
a vow many existences ago to become Buddhas, and
have lived ever since in such a way as to acquire
almost exhaustive stores of merit.[19] This merit is so
great that they could readily achieve the full status
of Buddhas and pass into *Nirvana*. Out of love and
pity, however, they postpone their entrance and
transfer their merit to those who call upon them in
prayer or give devotional thought to them. They sit
enthroned in the highest spiritual realms looking
down upon man, helping those who by faith seek
salvation.

Thus for one school the Buddha becomes a saint,
for the other a savior. In one school he is revered as
the sage, who, becoming enlightened, pointed man
to a way; in the other he is a compassionate being
who out of love for humanity postpones his entry into
Nirvana in order to transfer his merit to those who
need his help. We might say that the chief difference
between Theravada and Mahayana is that Mahayana

[19] Morgan, *op. cit.*, 395-396.

embraces the eternal Buddha while Theravada points to the historical Buddha.

There is still a schism in the Buddhist world between the two beliefs. The Theravada Buddhists claim that their doctrines derive from the teachings of Gautama himself and thus constitute the only true path, and the Mahayanists reply that the rigid teachings of the southern Buddhists are much too traditional and defensive. But upon the one figure in Buddhism they all agree, and that is the figure of the gentle sage who found the way to enlightenment. Whether it be Mahayana or Theravada Buddhism, every Buddhist firmly believes that it was the Buddha who remolded and revitalized a way of life which is to be applied universally, regardless of time, place, or prevailing culture. For in the words of Heinrich Zimmer, "the Mahayana, the big ferryboat, and Hinayana, the little, whether side by side or far apart, have together carried the millions of the Orient through centuries of transformation, secure in the understanding that the Buddha, somehow, in the most intimate, dependable way—no matter what their path of approach to him—was their indestructible, all-embracing Refuge." [20]

Heinrich Zimmer, *Philosophies of India* (Cleveland: The World Publishing Company, 1951), p. 1

CHAPTER SIX

The Straight Path of Islam

An angel or a god cannot set an example which man can follow. The dimensions would be utterly disparate. It is a curious inversion that a prophet's opponents often seek to justify their rejection of him on the ground that he is but a man, a single individual from among themselves. Yet, as the Quran points out, it is only a man who can serve as God's Messenger to men. An angel would be sent as a prophet if the earth were peopled with angels.[1]

"There is no god except God and Muhammad is the Apostle of God." These words form one of the shortest and most repeated creeds of any religion of mankind. This creed symbolizes with great simplicity and clarity the faith of almost five hundred million Muslims. But for the Western world it is one of the most misunderstood statements to be found in any of the major religions. The Muslim scriptures, the Quran or Koran,[2] is probably one of the most widely read

[1] Muhammad B. Khan, *Islam* (New York: Harper and Row, 1962), p. 73.

[2] "Koran" is the traditional spelling, although the Islamic word "Qur'an" more accurately suggests the real pronunciation. The Koran is divided into 114 chapters or "surahs" and is about four-fifths the length of the New Testament. Because the verses in the Koran do not follow in chronological order, most non-Muslims find the book difficult to read.

books in the world—certainly it is one of the most memorized—and yet no book is as foreign to Westerners. Though it is said that the name of Muhammad is given to more male children than any other in the world, and it is repeated as often as 40 times a day by the Islamic faithful; yet, among the major figures of history, the name and the figure behind it stand not only as one of the most complex but as one of the most controversial.

While Muhammad was one of the few religious founders to have grown up in the full light of history, so that we have more biographical details about him than other leaders, this has not narrowed the tremendous gap between the facts of his life and the results which we are just beginning to appreciate today. Though the basic concepts of Islam, as outlined in the Koran, are at most points identical with those of Judaism and Christianity, for centuries Muslims and Christians have been alienated from each other, partly by the fact that both have misunderstood the distinctive claims of each other's faiths.

To the Muslim, Islam *is* the religion of the God of the Old and the New Testament. The name "Islam" is said to mean "submission" and is derived from the word for "peace" *(salam)*. Muslims interpret it as meaning that perfect peace that comes when one's life is surrendered to God. An adherent of Islam is usually called a *Muslim* (of which the word "Moslem" is a Western adaptation). To the Muslim, *Islam* is a generic term applicable to every revealed religion, so long as that religion is not altered by men. For the Muslim this means that his religion did not begin with Muhammad in the seventh century A.D. but with God and the act of creation. The Koran speaks of the close relationship between its revelation and those of the Old and New Testaments: "God hath ordained for you [the Muslim] that religion which he commended unto Noah . . . unto Abraham and Moses and Jesus" (Surah 42:13). Thus "Islam" is the only religion acceptable to God, for "religion with God is Islam" (Surah 3:19).[3]

Stages of Revelation

The story of Islam, as aptly summed up by Wilfred C. Smith, the Islamic scholar at Harvard University, is that God did not leave man without witnesses of himself. In fact, revelation began when God created man. Man was intended to bear the impress of God's attributes and to be a living manifestation of his image (Surah 51:57). Islamic thought is more closely linked with Hebrew-Christian philosophy than that of Hinduism and Buddhism. In this sense, Islam is often thought of as a Western religion: it teaches that to achieve the end for which man was created, God gave him a pattern to follow. As soon as he was created, man was given guidance as to what God's requirements were.

In Islamic terms, Adam was the first messenger or prophet. Through Adam the human race was given the true message about God and the justice he wished established. Despite this guidance, man went his own way, living life for its own ends rather than for God's. While he was commanded to worship the one true God, he began to worship many gods. God had to intervene a second time in human history by send-

---

[3] Passages from the Koran are from Mohammed M. Pickthall, *The Meaning of the Glorious Koran* (New York: A Mentor Book, 1953).

ing Abraham and, through him, revealing once and for all the truth of God's oneness and sovereignty. Through faulty reason and willful error, man again faltered, and again God sent the messengers and the message to redeem men from their uncertainty. Time after time God chose messengers to reveal for their generation the truths men needed at that particular time and which they were able to grasp at that stage for the fulfillment of life. Some of the names of these messengers are forgotten, but some 28 of them have been preserved. Of those remembered, the most significant are Adam, Abraham, Moses, and Jesus.[4]

Islam says that, while Abraham gave the world the concept of monotheism, Moses gave groping humanity moral law as embodied in the Ten Commandments. In due time the law became obscured. Moses' followers lost much of the text. Some of it was corrupted; men kept adding to it. Furthermore, Islam says, the Jewish community believed that the divine commands applied only to themselves and thus corrupted the universality of one message intended for all mankind. Again, man found himself with only half-truths. Again, God sent another messenger, Jesus. Through Jesus, God revealed the Golden Rule. He showed men how to live with one another in love. But some who heard the message of Jesus, who himself was an "acceptor" like the other prophets before him, committed a major blunder. Instead of heeding Jesus' message, some of his followers came to worship the messenger instead. They actually called him the "Son of God"!

In Islam, much stress is laid on the belief in Jesus' virgin birth, his miracles, and his exemplary moral

[4] Wilfred C. Smith, *Islam in Modern History* (New York: A Mentor Book, 1957), pp. 18-20.

life, but he was, after all, Muslims believe, a human being.[5] To Jesus' utter amazement, Muslims say, his followers took his name and began to worship him and pray to him and ascribe to him the glory that belongs only to God. As the result of this folly, a community of believers calling themselves "Christians" arose and has existed through the centuries. It is Islam's contention that, though Christianity is superior to paganism in that it does not revere and worship a great number of deities, in the final analysis it is still polytheistic in that it does recognize and worship three persons as God. Furthermore, Islam believes that, by focusing its attention on Christ, the Christian community has neglected the full worship of God on the one hand, and on the other hand has neglected the moral order which God himself established "since they [the Christians] have cultivated personal piety but allowed social justice to slide, leaving the conduct of this-worldly affairs to 'secular' forces not under the dominion of the eternal norms. Though individually upright, they let history go its own way, unredeemed." [6]

But in one final, dramatic move, God intervened to give to men once and for all a message that would with undeviating precision guide him, and a messenger who would with scrupulous fidelity preserve his truth. A final prophet was needed, and God found him in Muhammad. Islam says that the creative element in God's intervention this time lay in the fact

---

[5] Islam considers Jesus a rather special being with a life attested by miracles, including that of his virgin birth (Surah 3:47 ff.). There is, as we have seen, the denial of his claims to divinity, as well as a denial of the crucifixion which is regarded as a Jewish fable. Muslims believe another man was crucified in Jesus' place.

[6] Wilfred C. Smith, op. cit., p. 21.

that Muhammad was able to apply God's truth as a "living embodiment in human history."

"Here was not only a restatement of what God has to say to us but a society developing around that restatement: a society that, grasping firmly the injunctions which are there revealed, dedicates itself to living according to them, and thereby sets forth on the reconstruction of human life on earth," writes Wilfred C. Smith.[7] Those who are willing to walk the "straight path," that is, accept that rightness or righteousness by which its behavior is patterned, are called "acceptors" or "submitters" (*Muslim* in Arabic). Islam believes that Muhammad's revelation was the last or the "seal" and represents the final step in the evolution of monotheistic religion, combining as it does the monotheism of the Hebrew prophets of the Old Testament and the universalism of Christianity; those who accept it are considered to be not only Muslims but *the* Muslims. Rejecting the nationalistic taint of Judaism and the Christology of Christianity, the Straight Path of Islam, the Muslim says, is universal and eternal and its laws are objectively valid; to live according to them is to find the reality in the universe.

Muhammad's Early Life

When Muhammad was born about 570 A.D. at Mecca in Arabia, the empires associated with the names of Egypt, Babylon, and Greece had already faded into history. Europe was still in the process of converting to Christianity; in South Asia, Hinduism and Buddhism had passed their golden era, and in China the philosophy of Confucius, which earlier

---

[7] *Ibid.*, pp. 22-23.

had been stirred by the advent of Buddhism, had begun a long, placid era. The two great Middle Eastern empires of Persia and Byzantium were engaged in a struggle which ultimately resulted in death for both. Religion, philosophy, and learning were at low ebb in Europe. In that part of the world the Dark Ages had begun, and mankind appeared to have entered upon a decline. Nowhere was this more evident than in Arabia, where the gloom was almost unrelieved.

The land of Muhammad's birth was barren; even the hardy and tolerant date palm did not prosper there. It has been said that though the wealth of three continents had poured endlessly into this place, "there were no gardens, and a stunted bush was an object of civic pride." The desert of Arabia was populated not only with warring tribes looking for food and fodder but, the inhabitants believed, with beastly spirits called *jinn,* a demonic group of demigods who roamed the desert at will. In the active imagination of the Arab, these spirits lived in the stones, rocks, caves, springs, and wells, and they struck terror in his heart. Polytheism and animism (the worship of spirits) ruled the day, and immorality ran rampant at religious convocations and fairs.

In Mecca was located the Kaaba, the holiest of shrines in Arabia, with 360 images of local and distant deities in its dark interior. Borrowing from the traditions of the Jewish community, the people of Mecca declared that the great patriarch Abraham, while on a visit to his son Ishmael, had built the Kaaba and had imbedded the black meteorite stone within it. From far and near across the desert, pilgrims came by the thousands to bow before it, to offer sacrifices of sheep and camels, to run the circuit of the stone seven times, and to hope for the blessings of heaven as the result of their religious fervor.

Perhaps the real factor which made Muhammad a prophet, says John Noss, was the fact that he early became an orphan, with an interest that was religious through and through. What made him a success, according to H. A. R. Gibb, the noted Arabic scholar, was the fact that he was born in Mecca.[8] Muhammad was a citizen of no mean city, in spite of the barrenness of Arabia. He was not at heart a Bedouin, nor did he share the ideas and outlook of the other wandering tribesmen; he was a citizen of a town whose inhabitants had acquired a wide knowledge of men and their ways in their commercial and diplomatic relations.

Muhammad was brought up in his uncle's family, one of the leading families in Mecca who shared in the care of the Kaaba. Prof. Mohammad Abd Allah Draz of Al Azhar University in Cairo retells the early life of Mohammad.[9] As a young orphan he came to be called Muhammad, or "highly praised." When he was 25 he entered the service of a rich widow called Khadija, his senior by 15 years. He conducted her affairs as a trade agent in the caravan business so well that he soon became her steward and then her husband. The marriage, despite the disparity in age and affluence, proved to be happy. For 26 years, until her death, she was a devoted wife and a constant source of comfort and support to him.

Because of this marriage, Muhammad was free of

---

[8] See especially Chapter I of Gibb's *Mohammedanism* (New York: Oxford University Press, 1962).

[9] Kenneth W. Morgan (ed.), *Islam—The Straight Path* (New York: The Ronald Press, 1958), pp. 6-21.

economic worry and able to devote himself more and more to the religious impulse that was so much a part of him. As he studied the various religions and their practices, Muhammad would often fall into fits of melancholy. The purpose of religion was to explain the mystery of life and death, of the heavens and all they contained, the problem of evil, of punishment and reward, he felt, but people found different solutions to this mystery. Where did the truth lie? Muhammad thought deeply about it. He was often seen leaving town and seeking a lonely spot where he could think undisturbed. One such spot, a cave called Hira in a hill outside Mecca, became his favorite haunt. He sat there for hours and sometimes for days, meditating upon the mysteries of good and evil, unable to accept the idolatry and superstition and cruelty of his day; this great burning mind and this great seething, simmering heart was reaching out to God.

God's Apostle

One day in his 40th year, as he was lying in a trance inside the cave at Hira with his mind locked in deepest contemplation, he received his commission as an apostle of God. Gautama pierced the secret of the universe through intense inward concentration; Muhammad received his insight through a voice which he said came directly from God through a messenger of revelation, the archangel Gabriel. The voice and a vision of light which seemed to fill "the horizon from end to end," said, "Muhammad! Cry!" Twice the voice of the archangel spoke out, and twice Muhammad refused to heed it, wishing nothing so much as to escape from its sound. "Cry!" commanded the voice for the third time. "What shall I cry?"

Muhammad asked in desperation. The answer came back:

"Read [cry]: in the name of thy Lord who createth,
Createth man from a clot.
Read: And thy Lord is the Most Bounteous.
Who teacheth by the pen,
Teacheth man that which he knew not"

(Surah 96:1-4).

When the vision ended, Muhammad, though unable to read or write, was able to recite all of Surah or Chapter 96 of the Koran, of which only the first lines are given here. According to Prof. Draz, this was the first fragment of the Koran. Muhammad rushed home in great excitement, half doubting, half believing. Was he losing his sanity? He told Khadija that he was either "possessed" of the *jinn* or he really had been commissioned a prophet. Later he was to defend the authenticity of his experience with the words: "Then he [the messenger of the revelation] drew nigh and came down till he was (distant) two bow's lengths or even nearer, and he revealed unto his slave that which he revealed. The heart lied not (in seeing) what it saw. Will ye then dispute with him concerning what he seeth?" (Surah 53:8-12). The voice came back again and again and its command was always the same: "Preach."

From this point on Muhammad's life was no longer his own. He so impressed Khadija with his sincerity that she became his first convert, and Muslims often remark that this speaks well for the genuineness of his experience, for no one knows a man as thoroughly as his wife. From that time forth, Muhammad gave himself to God and to man. He began preaching with unswerving purpose in the face of relentless

insults and outrage. Though his followers were im-
prisoned, pelted with stones, starved, and exposed to
the heat of the desert, Muhammad never ceased
preaching the words which he believed God was
transmitting to him until his death 23 years later.

Muhammad attracted only a small band of adherents in the early years of his preaching. His fellow
townsmen would have none of him, for his activity
was beginning to cut off the funds that people from
all over Arabia normally brought to Mecca on their
pilgrimage to the Kaaba. They sought to quiet him,
but Muhammad would not be silenced, nor would
he traffic in human weakness. To those who came to
him seeking a sign or a miracle, he said that God had
not sent him to work wonders but to preach to a
miracle-hungry, idolatrous generation. He claimed
no supernatural powers. He emphasized again and
again that he was a man like the rest: "I am only a
mortal like you. My Lord inspireth in me that your
God is only One God. And whoever hopeth for the
meeting with his Lord, let him do righteous work,
and make none sharer of the worship due unto his
Lord" (Surah 18:111).

The *Hijrah*

Before the Meccan leaders were able to do away
with the "driveller, star-gazer, and maniac-poet" in
their midst, help came to Muhammad from an unexpected source. A group of pilgrims from Yathrib [10]
in the north had heard Muhammad preach and were
impressed. The city was facing internal troubles and

---

[10] In honor of the prophet, Yathrib changed its name to Medinat-
un-Nabe, "The City of the Prophet," and then later, by contrac-
tion, to Medina, "The City."

was in need of a strong leader. Muhammad and his followers were invited to come to Medina and make it their home, with the assurance that they would be treated as brothers, that the precepts of Islam would be observed, and that none but God would be worshiped there. When the Meccans became aware of this, they sought to keep Muhammad from escaping, but he eluded them by hiding for two nights in a cave with a companion. Horsemen scouring the countryside came so close that his companion feared for their lives. When he mentioned his fear and the fact that they were only two, the prophet replied: "Grieve not. Lo! God is with us" (Surah 9:40). This event, the *Hijrah* or *Hegira* (The Flight), took place in 622 A.D. The Muslim calendar begins with this year which is regarded by Muslims as the founding date of their religion and the turning point in world history.

On the face of it, there was almost every reason why the Medina venture should have failed. It proved, however, to be one of the world's great success stories. The man who had fled his native city, harassed by people who wanted to take his life, arrived at another city scarcely 200 miles away to translate his theory of religious community into practice. Modest though his beginning was, it proceeded with increasing vitality, for it became evident that here was not simply a body of private religious beliefs, but a community seeking its own system of government, laws, and institutions.

Given unrestricted power over the town, Muhammad immediately set about evolving a new system of religious practices and cultures. A house of worship was erected—the first mosque. Weekly services on Friday were begun; prostration during prayer (at

first toward Jerusalem, to please the Jewish community, but when the Jews refused conversion, then
toward Mecca) was required, and a call to prayer
from the mosque's roof (at first only for the Friday
services, and then every day) was established. Col-
lection of alms for the poor and support of the
prophet were among other practices which soon were
established. After seven years of struggle, Mecca, the
intellectual and political capital of Arabia, became
an enthusiastic partner in Muhammad's plans. Islam,
the "surrender," had come into being. A new world
power was born.

When Muhammad died in 632 A.D. (10 A.H. or
after *Hijrah*), virtually all of Arabia was under his
control. He had succeeded in uniting his country-
men as had no other Arab before him. Within a
century after the founding of Islam, the followers of
Muhammad became the masters of an empire greater
than that of Rome at its zenith. In this period they
"assimilated to their creed, speech, and even physical types, more aliens than any stock before or since,
not excepting the Hellenic, the Roman, the Anglo-
Saxon, or the Russian," [11] according to the Arabic
historian Philip Hitti.

In less than 100 years, Muhammad's followers established and took responsibility for a new order that
extended deep into Asia and far into Africa, a thousand and more miles from its starting point. Within
six years of Muhammad's death all Syria and Persia
(now Iraq) became tributaries; in four more years
Egypt was added to the new Muslim empire, and by
the first third of the eighth century the Arabs had
spread into Morocco, Spain, France, to the gates of

---

[11] Philip Hitti, *History of the Arabs* (London: Macmillan and Co.,
Ltd., 1940), p. 4.

Constantinople, far across central Asia, and to the Indus River in what is now West Pakistan.

If Arab forces had not been defeated by the Frankish king Charles Martel in the Battle of Tours in France in 732 A.D., the entire western world today might be Muslim, as Spain was for 700 years. Thus within his brief span of mortal life, Muhammad had established a religion which in vast areas superseded Christianity and Judaism and still claims the adherence of one out of every six to seven persons in the world. Its call to prayer rings out through most of the 24 hours of the day, encircling the larger portion of the globe within the crescent from Indonesia to Morocco. The success of Islam does not surprise the Muslim. The past president of the General Assembly of the United Nations sums up the sentiments of the faithful: "Islam sets forth and places at man's disposal a most effective and potent means of achieving the purpose of life. Of all God's numberless bounties bestowed upon man, it is one of the greatest and most precious, and it is indispensable for the beneficent growth of man in the epoch now unfolding before him." [12]

The Koran

In spite of the great admiration, respect, and affection which the devout Muslim feels for Muhammad—he will not mention the prophet's name without the benediction, "Peace be unto him!"—Muslims never mistake him for a god or even for the earthly pillar of their faith. This place is reserved for Islam's scripture, the Koran. Islam says Muhammad was a human

---

[12] Kahn, *op. cit.*, p. 211.

being, no more, no less, and because of this he could serve as an example for mankind. He possessed and claimed no supernatural powers. The only miracle Muhammad claimed was the Koran, which God dictated directly to him, he said, and which his followers memorized and later wrote down for him.

Many Christians have difficulty understanding Islam because they misunderstand the role of Muhammad. Their error lies in supposing that the roles of Jesus in Christianity and Muhammad in Islam are comparable. Wilfred C. Smith reminds us that more insight is gained if one realizes that the roles of Paul and Muhammad are more comparable. Both were apostles; Paul preached a message, as did Muhammad. The person of Jesus in Christianity corresponds to the Koran in Islam, not to Muhammad. For the Muslim "the Word" has been made incarnate in history and "has dwelt among us," but in the Koran.[13] Christians have also misunderstood Muhammad's attitude toward the Christian community. Muhammad held both the Jewish and the Christian communities in considerable esteem because he was aware that they possessed their own scriptures. Throughout the Koran these communities bear the title "People of the Book," and therefore these people are regarded as highly privileged because they possess revelations from God.

In regard to Christ, the Koran makes statements that it makes of no other prophet and places him on a level higher than the prophets who preceded him. He was born of a virgin; he performed miracles; he was raised by God from the dead. He did not, however, die on the cross, according to the Koran. Mu-

---

[13] Wilfred C. Smith, *op. cit.*, pp. 25-26, footnote 13.

hammad denied the Lord's crucifixion, but not with
contempt. He denied it as a warning to the Jewish
community who boasted that it had put one of God's
prophets to death. Out of the esteem which Muhammad held for one of God's prophets, he rebelled
against this claim the only way he knew how—by
denying it. Thus the Koran states: "And they crucified him not!" (Surah 4:156).

The Koran remains the pillar of Islam's faith. In
the Koran God makes himself and his purpose known
to man in the form of words. Words are supremely
important in Islamic religious life. "No people in the
world," writes Philip Hitti, "are so moved by the
word, spoken, or written, as the Arabs." [14] No language seems as capable of exercising such influence
over its users as Arabic, with an alphabet that, next
to the Latin, is the most widely used in the world.
And of no words is this more true than those Muslims
believe were dictated by God's messenger to Muhammad and incorporated into the Koran. The Koran
was revealed in Arabic, and while interpretations,
such as Mohammad M. Picthall's *The Meaning of
the Glorious Koran,* appear in other languages, to
translate it is to betray its divine source, the Muslim says. Those who read the Koran in the original
Arabic speak of its terse, rich, forceful language,
striking, soaring, vivid, terrible, tender, and breath-
taking. Such adjectives as "beautiful" or "persua-
sive" are not generally applied to the Koran, for they
have no meaning in the light of its "flashing images
that go directly to the mind and produce its power-
fully hypnotic spell." A skilled reciter of the Koran

---

[14] Huston Smith, *Religions of Man* (New York: A Mentor Book,
1959), p. 211.

can reduce an Arabic-speaking audience to tears and ecstasy, and for 13 centuries Arabic has been considered the true accents of the Eternal.

"It is not difficult to surmise why this is so. Nomads are prohibited by their transient way of life from developing visual art. Their architecture is restricted to flapping tents, their crafts to the few pots and fabrics they can carry with them. With life one long process of packing and unpacking, one is not likely to accumulate a museum. Blocked on the visual side by the need to keep gear light, the nomad's art took a verbal turn. 'Wisdom,' says a famous adage, 'has alighted on three things: the brain of the Franks, the hands of the Chinese, and the tongue of the Arabs.' " [15]

The teachings of Muhammad, as set down in the Koran, became the creed of Islam with few additions or alterations. The difference in interpretation and method which gave rise to the sects of Islam were not marked by rejection of the words Muhammad received in revelation. As one becomes acquainted with the fundamentals of the faith as set forth in the Koran, one realizes how closely it resembles a simplified version of Judaism and Christianity. The Koran indicates that Muhammad had considerable contact with some of the Jewish communities in his land, especially in Medina after his flight. Muhammad seems to have become fairly well acquainted with the content of the Jewish scriptures. This becomes evident when we note that more than 500 Koranic texts mention the names of Noah, Abraham, and Moses. The situation is different with respect to New Testament writings. The name of Jesus appears in

[15] *Ibid.*, pp. 211-212.

93 surahs or chapters, but the Koran never mentions the Apostle Paul or refers to any of the Epistles. It would seem, then, that judging from the Koran Muhammad had little or no contact with individual Christians during his lifetime.

At any rate, the fundamental theological concepts of Islam are at many points identical with those of Judaism and Christianity, unlike the concepts of Hinduism or Buddhism. These concepts have been made very simple and appear to be within the understanding of all. There is no need for the believer to puzzle his head over subtleties. The way of life recommended to him has little to do with theory or speculation and much to do with practice—definite things to do each day to assure his salvation. Salvation is by faith, but faith in the validity of works; faith in God and in the rightness of what he has set as a pattern for mankind. A Muslim is not asked to agree, for there is not much to agree to; he is asked to submit. He is asked to walk the Straight Path, the pattern for man which God has outlined.

Five Pillars of Islam

The content of the Straight Path outlines a system of life covering economic, political, social, and religious matters. An essential part of Islam is obeying these laws. In practical matters such as marriage, for example, Islamic law permits a man five wives—provided they are treated equally—for the relationship between man and woman must be one of equality. Man's span of life is predetermined, the Muslim believes, but he does not think of this as a denial of his freedom. Indeed, he believes that on the Day of Resurrection and Judgment he must face God as

judge to account for his deeds and to be rewarded
according to his merits. The dead shall also rise from
their graves. Man's happiness or unhappiness in the
hell or paradise of the next world depends upon the
manner in which he observes God's laws in this
world. The principles upon which the Islamic way
of life rests have come to be known as the Five Pillars. The content of the Straight Path is embodied in
these principles.[16]

The first pillar is Islam's creed: "There is no God
but God and Muhammad is God's Apostle." To repeat this creed at least once during a lifetime is to become a Muslim. Actually, however, this formula is in
constant use and repeated by practicing Muslims
many times each day and heard everywhere in the
Muslim world. As with the Jews, the declaration of
the unity of God is the most important article in the
creed. Muslims object to Christianity because in
Christianity, they say, "God is the third of three."
Islam teaches that God is one—omnipresent, majestic, awesome, merciful, and many other things, but
for the Muslim there is no greater affirmation than
"he is one." The Koran directs men to turn their
thoughts from the fruitless attempt to know the essence of his ultimate reality. God is simply one.
Every other sin may be forgiven man but not that of
shirk, the ascribing of partners to God or the failure
to recognize that the final truth and power of the
universe is one. There is no God but *Allah.* The word

---

[16] For an insightful discussion on "Islamic Beliefs and Code of
Law," see Prof. Mahmud Shaltout's chapter in Kenneth W. Mor-
gan (ed.), *Islam, The Straight Path* (New York: The Ronald
Press, 1958), pp. 87-143. Prof. Shaltout is a member of the Body
of the Grand Ulama and professor of comparative law at Al Azhar
University, Cairo, Egypt.

"Allah" is formed by joining the definite article *al* (the) with *Illah* (God). *Allah,* then, is not another name for God but means *the* God.[17] "And Muhammad is His Apostle" (or messenger or prophet).

It seems self-evident to Muslims that God must reveal himself through prophets. Muhammad, they believe, was the last and the greatest of them all; none has been his equal because none has received or handed down so perfect and final a revelation. The Muslim's confidence in Muhammad's revelation is not decreased by the fact that his teaching was neither new nor original. The Muslim holds that the Koran completes and fulfills the half-truths that other religions only haltingly declared. To say Muhammad is God's apostle is to assert that the message revealed to Muhammad is authentic. If anyone believes this, then he is "accepting" as binding the practical duties that flow from this revelation and are given in the Straight Path. He is recognizing the obligation to perform them because they are not of human origin but divine.

The second pillar in Islam's faith is prayer (Surah 29:45), an experience of communion with the divine. The devout Muslim reserves time each day for five acts of devotion *(Salat),* at dawn, noon, mid-afternoon, sunset, and nightfall. In city, country, or on the desert, the Muslim is required to go through a ritual of ablution, roll out his prayer rug, bow down toward Mecca, and offer to God a witness of his faith and a declaration of praise and submission to his will. It is

[17] Kenneth Cragg argues that since both Christian and Muslim faiths believe in "one supreme sovereign Creator—god," they are referring, by whatever terms used for him, to the same Being. See *The Call of the Minaret* (New York: Oxford University Press, 1956), pp. 36-37.

common simply to repeat the Arabian "Lord's Prayer" found in the opening surah of the Koran. Occasions for private prayers are numberless during the day, and Muslims do not recognize a Sabbath or Sunday, for the daily hours replace the holy day. Friday, however, comes the closest to a "holy" day, for on this day a special service of public prayer is conducted. Huston Smith remarks that those who have seen the faithful in prayer testify that one of the most impressive sights in the religions of man occurs when, during the ritual prayer, the worshipers silently follow their leader or *imam*, standing erect when he does, inclining the head and body and dropping on their knees when he does, placing their hands upon the ground and putting their foreheads to the pavement in prostration at the exact moment they see him do so.[18]

After the prayers on Friday, a sermon is preached on Muslim doctrine. Since there are no clergy or ecclesiastical ranks among Muslims, anyone who is capable can lead prayers, deliver sermons, and present lectures. The leader or *imam* who assumes this role is generally recognized as knowledgeable and one of the better-informed Muslims. When a mosque is not easily available, services are held in private rooms, in an open park, in a university classroom, in the desert, on board a vessel at sea, and even in a train. Worshipers participating in the service face toward the Kaaba in Mecca, a gesture which makes them feel part "of one history and one solidarity." The call to prayer is made by the *muezzin* from the minaret by word of mouth. There are no bells or

---

[18] Cragg, *op. cit.*, p. 219. Each daily *salat* or act of prayer has its own stipulated number of ritual "bowings," also. See also Cragg, *op. cit.*, pp. 107-108.

trumpets, for the sound of words, as we have seen, has in itself a magnetic, drawing power and plays a vital part in Islam.

> God is great (four times); I bear witness that there is no being worthy of worship save God (twice); I bear witness that Muhammad is the apostle of God (twice); come to prayer (twice); come to salvation (twice); God is great (twice); there is no being worthy of worship save God (once).

Whoever hears the melodious, resonant "God is great" is reminded that he is to transfer his attention from the business at hand to the worship of God, which is the ultimate purpose and fulfillment of his being.

> It may be thought that five services daily is a little too much and may become burdensome. In fact, that is not so. It is a matter of comparative values. All five services taken together do not take up more than about two hours—no more time than a person in the West may spend watching television. In the eyes of a Muslim, a diversion such as television, or the formalities attendant upon a ceremonial dinner, together with the preparations concerning dress, etc., that go with it, or a rubber of bridge has little value, whereas participation in congregational worship is nutriment for the soul. It can be, and in most cases is, a cathartic experience.[19]

The third pillar of the Muslim faith is the obligation to give alms or the practice of charity (*Zakat*). This term is usually translated "alms," but it is distinguished from free-will offerings. The *Zakat* constitutes the principle of social responsibility by which the possession of wealth obligates the possessor to

---

[19] Khan, *op. cit.*, p. 103.

concern himself with those who lack what he enjoys. *Zakat* in Arabic really means "that which purifies" or "that which fosters." According to the Koran, all real sources of wealth, such as the sun, the moon, the stars, the earth, and the clouds, are the gifts of God to the whole of mankind. Wealth is produced by the application of man's skill and labor to the resources which have been provided by God and over which man enjoys only proprietary rights. In the wealth that is produced, therefore, three parties are entitled to a share: the workman, the individual who supplies the capital, and the community, representing the whole of mankind. The community's share in produced wealth is called the *Zakat*. After this has been set aside, the rest is "purified" and may be divided among the remaining parties entitled to share in it.

The levy or *Zakat* is usually assessed on both income and capital and figured at 2½ percent. The proceeds of the tax, or more properly of the "loan made to God," are devoted to relieving poverty, winning over the cooperation of those who have not adjusted their lives to the Islamic system, helping people in debt, providing comfort for travelers, and, generally, to any community effort such as public health, public works, medical services, and educational endeavors. It thus fosters the welfare of the community. The 2½ percent levy may seem minimal, compared with the tithe of Christianity and Judaism. The levy, however, as Muhammad Z. Khan remarks, is assessed on both capital and income. While the money contributed to Christianity and Judaism is generally devoted to the maintenance of buildings and religious institutions, in Islam the contributions go almost entirely to the relief of human need. "To have is to share"; "only giving cleanses keeping"; "property is a trust"—as these precepts are followed, the Islamic good becomes a reality in human society. The Koran lays down the rule for the faithful: "Those who spread their wealth by night and day, by stealth and openly, verily their reward is with their Lord, and there shall no fear come upon them neither shall they grieve" (Surah 2:274).

The fourth pillar of the Muslim faith is the ordinance enjoying fasting. This fast is held in the month of *Ramadan* (Islam's holy month), which commemorates the year in which the Koran was revealed and the month when, 10 years later, Muhammad made his initial flight *(Hijrah)* from Mecca to Medina. Except for the sick and ailing, the aged and the pregnant, nursing mothers and travelers, the fast is an obligation required by the Koran of all who have attained the age of accountability (Surah 2:184). During *Ramadan* all Muslims abstain from food and drink and sexual intercourse from dawn to sunset. Food is eaten during the hours of darkness only. At dawn, after it is light enough to distinguish between a white and black thread, nothing is eaten until sundown, when again the difference between the threads is no longer distinguishable (Surah 2:187). The month of fasting is a lunar month coming 10 days earlier every year and thus rotating through the year in cycles of approximately 33 years so that in every part of the world it falls in all seasons in turn. In the tropics, when the month falls during the summer, the fast entails considerable hardship because normal work must be carried on in the intense heat without so much as a drop of water. However, the fast is not looked upon as a penance but rather as a physical and spiritual discipline.

The Koran speaks of fasting in Surah 2:183: "Fasting is prescribed for you even as it was prescribed for those before you, that ye may ward off evil." It is right to fast at any time, but traditionally it is 30 times better to fast during *Ramadan* than at any other time. Several blessings accrue to those involved in the act of fasting. The fast places everybody, rich and poor alike, on the same level. The well-to-do experience the pangs of hunger and thirst with their less-favored brothers and sisters, so that hunger becomes an experience shared in common. Furthermore, the observance of its regulations gives the Muslim an opportunity to intensify his own communion with God. During *Ramadan* more time is generally devoted to the study of the Koran than at any other time. For the last 10 days of the holy month some people stay in the mosque continuously and devote all their time to studying the Koran and to the remembrance of God, meditating upon his attributes and the manner of their manifestation.

Like the act of submission in prayer, the faithful Muslim becomes aware that the act of fasting helps keep life in its proper perspective. What is significant in the fast is the assertion that man has larger needs than bread, that his body is to be his servant and not his master, and that ordered, voluntary privation is not a penance but a discipline. Indeed, Kenneth Cragg writes that the fast, which ends with a feast on the first day of the following month, resembles certain features of the West's Christmas season. It is a time of general desire after better things. There is a giving of gifts symbolizing mutual affection, and there is a great surge of satisfaction and aspiration which, for Muslims, ends an exacting discipline.

The pilgrimage, or *Hajj*, the fifth pillar of Islam, makes Mecca the focal point of a yearly homage that often represents for the Muslim the aspiration of a lifetime. Once in a lifetime every Muslim man or woman is expected to make his or her way to Mecca. The Koran points out that honoring what has been declared sacred—in this case, the Kaaba whose many idols Muhammad destroyed—promotes righteousness of heart (Surah 22:31, 33). It is natural for the Muslim to look to Mecca and the Kaaba in devotion, for it was the first house consecrated to the worship of the one true God (Surah 3:96). Abraham and Ishmael themselves, according to the Koran, raised the foundations of the house (Surah 2:127).

How Abraham happened to journey to Mecca is an interesting part of Islamic history. The descendants of Adam included Noah, who had a son named Shem. Shem became the father of the "Semites" (literally, descendants of Shem) and, like the Jews, the Arabs regard themselves as a Semitic people. Shem's descendant, Abraham, married Sarah. She was unable to bear Abraham a son, so he took Hagar for his wife as well. Hagar bore Abraham a son called Ishmael, and shortly thereafter Sarah bore a son called Isaac. Thereupon Sarah demanded that Abraham banish Ishmael and Hagar from the tribe. According to the Koranic account, Ishmael went to Mecca; his descendants grew up in Arabia and are Muslims, whereas those of Isaac, who remained in Palestine, are Jews.

Muslims believe that when Abraham was on one of his visits to Ishmael he and his son built the first house of worship. Upon its erection he was commanded to "proclaim unto mankind the Pilgrimage; they will come to thee on foot and on every lean camel; they will come from every deep ravine" (Surah 22:27). The pilgrimage thus begun through

Abraham has through the centuries become a well-recognized religious institution. The object of the pilgrimage is to give Muslims the opportunity to join with fellow Muslims from all over the world in the worship of God, in the offering of sacrifices, in the fulfilling of their vows of piety, and in performing the circuits of the Kaaba while glorifying and praising God. Since Muhammad's day, all pilgrims who have entered the sacred precincts of Mecca have worn the same kind of seamless white garments. The wearing of the pilgrim's garb is a "leveling practice" by which people of all countries and languages are made to feel like brothers and are able to mingle with one another without distinction or race or class. The pilgrimages seek to provide a useful service in international relations, for they bring together people from various countries, demonstrating to them and to the world that their loyalty as Muslims transcends the loyalties of their national boundaries. H. A. R. Gibb sums up the importance of this annual event by stating:

> The significance of the Pilgrimage in maintaining the spiritual vitality and the communal life of Islam has been incalculable. The hardships (and frequently even dangers) which it evolved for the ordinary believer, the personal spiritual experience and the sense of community reinforced by participation in common rituals and worship with a multitude of fellow-Muslims from many lands—all these gave a new dimension to his understanding of and personal identification with the Faith, besides earning him the coveted title of *Al-Hajj* or *Hajji*.[20]

---

[20] R. C. Zaehner, *The Concise Encyclopedia of Living Faiths* (New York: Hawthorn Books, Inc., 1959), p. 185.

The number of pilgrims on the *hajj* has increased greatly in recent years. There was a time when observers of Islam expressed fear that, as a religion, Islam was becoming weakened in body as well as in soul. Some have said that as a faith and as a concrete, historical body of law and community it could not exist in modern civilization, for it had withdrawn intellectually for too long from any real engagement with alien thought. Twentieth century nationalism, however, has brought new independence and a new spirit of confidence to the countries, especially of Africa and Asia, where Islamic majorities are dominant. New governments within Islam with its simple proclamation of the Straight Path and the Five Pillars are helping to revive its long-dormant zeal for converts. And the continuing lure of the *hajj* makes it clear that the spirit of Muhammad's faith will not be so easily quenched. Islam will probably have to undergo the same kind of transition that Christianity went through, as the concept of Christendom fell before secularization. In time Islam may lose its overtones of an ideology governing all of life, as Christianity did in the Middle Ages, to become stripped down and freshened—simply one of man's many ways of encountering and dealing with the mystery of God.

CHAPTER SEVEN

Learning from Other Faiths

The new approach in the study of the religions is that of engagement, personal involvement in something which is of deep concern to millions of our fellow human beings.

This is an exacting, indeed almost a terrifying approach. Can one launch oneself into the heart and spirit of another religion without disloyalty to one's own?[1]

The question being asked today is no longer whether we can learn from the other religions or even *what* we can learn from them: the question is, *how* are we going to learn from them? When the points of agreement as well as the differences between religions are uncovered, how are we to come to grips with the issues involved in this learning process? In the past there has been little disposition among the believers of the world religions to learn from one another, but this is changing. Today there is a new openness and almost an eagerness to learn not only about other religions but to learn from them.

[1] Stephen Neill, *Christian Faith and Other Faiths* (London: Oxford University Press, 1961), pp. 4, 5.

For the Christian this poses fundamental questions: Stephen Neill, the perceptive Christian apologist, has asked the hard questions:[2] Can the Christian become deeply involved in another man's religion without being unfaithful to his own? Does not such a spirit of detachment loosen one's adherence to his own faith? The question in the mind of the Christian is: Can he learn from Hinduism, Buddhism, Islam, and other religions and still remain loyal to the faith of his fathers and to the faith which gives meaning to his own existence? He cannot go back on Jesus Christ and still be Christian; can he, then, *really* learn anything from what is most vital to men of other creeds and practices?

The study of the religions has shown us that the risk of losing one's own faith as the result of seeking insight into another man's faith is not nearly as dangerous an adventure as was first believed. We have long since recognized that religion cannot be studied in a vacuum and that a commitment to one's own faith renders a man more, not less, sensitive to the commitment of others whose beliefs about God may differ widely and whose faith finds different forms of expressions. The study of the history of the religions has shown that those who have the deepest and most confident faith themselves are the ones who have the courage to launch out on this adventure of the human spirit. The Christian today must "put himself to school" with other faiths in readiness to believe that they have something to teach him. However, the man for whom Jesus Christ is "the way, the truth, and the life" cannot compromise on that and remain Christian.

---

[2] Neill, *op. cit.*, pp. 17, 18.

As we seek greater insights into other faiths, how shall we learn from them? Here we can cite two examples of how this learning might take place; then we will close this chapter with a look into the future for what the study of other religions might imply, especially for the Christian.

Buddhist Compassion, Christian Love

Most of the world is familiar with the picture of the Buddha as the Compassionate One. Throughout Buddhist countries, the Enlightened One is held up as the symbol of great compassion and as worthy of being emulated by his followers. Can the Christian who also has a concept of compassion, in this case called love or *agape* in the Greek of the New Testament, learn anything from his Buddhist friends? How can the Buddhist learn from his Christian neighbors? Is the concept of Buddhist compassion and of Christian *agape* the same? Is there anything distinctive in Christ's kind of love, compared with Buddha's kind of compassion? To carry this one step farther, is Christian love the same as liking people or relating to and identifying with them?

The Christian and the Buddhist say that one does not have to be either a Buddhist or a Christian to like people; one only has to be human. This kind of humanity expresses itself in human kindness throughout the world. It is human to like people and identify with them. When an accident happens on a city street, a crowd gathers, not just out of curiosity but out of a sense of wanting to help. When disaster strikes a family, the whole neighborhood joins in to help. When people are sick, others visit them, take them flowers, and extend their best wishes for a speedy recovery. There is an enormous flow of kindness and general goodwill among human beings. In the case of America, people of other lands say that with all the faults America may have, she is one of the most generous nations in the world. Americans love to help, but then people the world over have their community chests, Red Cross organizations, cancer societies, and a multiplicity of other welfare agencies. Most people know how to help, and most people love to help, sometimes in large material ways. It does not take saints to want to help people; it takes only human beings.

Is there a difference, then, between loving people in the Christian sense and having compassion on them in the Buddhist sense, or simply helping them in the human sense? What is the basic difference between the Buddhist concept of compassion and the Christian concept of *agape* on the one hand, and on the other, the human disposition for wanting to give and feeling good about helping people? In the New Testament the word *agape* is used for the first time in a radically different sense. It refers to the kind of love God has for man, love that reaches from the higher to the lower, love that all men are urged to have for one another, whether they are friends or enemies, accepted or rejected, liked or disliked. It is the kind of love that reaches down as a father reaches down to lift up his small son who cannot quite reach up to him. It is a need as simple as this that the Christian feels in relation to God. When he does the reaching up, he cannot get there; God must reach down to him. And because he has reached down to him in Jesus Christ, there is a "given-ness" about this kind of love that transcends the human sense of it. He who has received *agape*—the New

Testament speaks of it as a gift—receives also the un-
acceptable and the unlovable, and not only accepts
but seeks to transform.

The word "love" in the Christian sense has an element of longing in it. There is a longing to bring one's
neighbor to a different and newer level, a longing to
see beneath the surface needs of people to their real
needs, to take them not at face value but at their
heart's value, a longing to lift them up and to point
them in the direction of the kingdom of God. The
need of *agape* is the need to lift the beloved beyond
himself or herself. The success of this attempt is not
the prerequisite of *agape* but its consequence. Christian love seeks to accept and to transform by taking
the needs of people and channeling them into the
stream of God's grace and power. There is always
"the will to transform the other one either directly,
or indirectly by transforming the sociological and
psychological structures by which he is condi-
tioned." [3]

The difference between the Buddhist concept of
compassion and the Christian concept of *agape* lies
in this area of transformation. Buddhism does not
wish, nor does it think it necessary, to seek the transformation of another. Paul Tillich said that compassion is a state in Buddhism in which "he who does
not suffer under his own conditions may suffer by
identification with another who does not suffer." [4]
He who does not suffer neither accepts the suffering
out of pity for the one who is suffering, nor does he

---

[3] Paul Tillich, *Christianity and the Encounter of the World Religions* (New York: Columbia University Press, 1963), p. 71. See
his chapter on "A Christian-Buddhist Conversation," especially
part IV.

[4] *Ibid.*, p. 71.

try to transform the suffering of the individual, but he suffers his suffering through identification. This compassion, however, does not emphasize personal attachments. Buddhism believes that to act primarily in terms of practical helpfulness to individuals is a mistake, or at least a lower order of spiritual action. Individuals are not real or lasting, since the universe is impersonal, "populated by streams of being that endlessly perpetuate themselves in newly individual forms, rather than by genuinely unique persons." [5]

Detached benevolence in Buddhism represents a higher order of spiritual action, an active compassion and an immediate kind of love which seeks to fill human need by relating one's self in an impersonal way to another. The movement in Buddhism is not "a reaching down and a bringing up" to a higher and newer level of reality but it is a "reaching out." Its goal is not the transformation of reality; its goal is salvation *from* reality. Prof. Hajime Nakamura of the University of Tokyo says that as the Buddhist meditates on the "self," his own self and the selves of others are dissolved into a conglomeration of impersonal elements. By dissolving one's existence into component parts, the individual rids himself of the notion of self and he then is led to a limitless expansion of the self because he identifies with more and more living beings. [6]

The Christian may learn something from this contrast. He may, as he comes to a deepened under-

[5] Winston L. King, *Buddhism and Christianity* (Westminster Press. Copyright © 1962, W. J. Jenkins), p. 98. See also Ch. III, pp. 64-102.

[6] Kenneth W. Morgan (ed.), *The Path of the Buddha* (New York: The Ronald Press, 1956), p. 387.

standing of *agape,* recognize that what is represented
as "Christian love" in his churches seldom resembles
the new meaning the New Testament gives to the
word. In fact, he may be hard pressed to recognize
the difference between Christian love and Buddhist
compassion. At any rate, he will want to be doubly
sure that his words about *agape* somehow are reflected in the "doing" of it. When the New Testament speaks of *agape,* it is speaking of participation
in a man's life with a creative kind of love that
Christians claim to be the kind of love that overcomes
the world.

The Christian may thus learn from his Buddhist
friend how easy it is to make pronouncements about
agape, but how difficult it is to have enough of the
"given" in his life so that a difference is made in it.
He may be made more keenly aware that much of
what has been represented as the Christian's unique
kind of love may simply be the natural inclination
"to do good," without any thought of pointing men
and women in the direction of the kingdom of God.
Then he may realize how easy it is for his words to
become divorced from his experience, and may examine more closely the basis of his own faith and the
grounds of his own life. Because of this encounter he
may be more aware than ever of his need for God,
and thus he will have learned and profited from another religion.

Divine Descent and Incarnation

When we turn to a consideration of the Hindu concept of divine descent and the Christian doctrine of
the incarnation, we have another example from
which to learn, this time from Hinduism. We have

noted previously that the stories, parables, and legends in Hinduism may or may not have a historical basis; it really does not make any difference to the Hindu. The abstract and subtle ideas of his religious system are conveyed through them. Thus it is commonly said among Hindus that it makes no difference whether Rama or Krishna or Christ or any other manifestation of God ever lived; mankind can still profit by what they are reported to have said or taught. No one really knows what the real Krishna was like or even if there was such a person. The Christian, on the other hand, finds great significance in history, and the historicity of certain events are of great importance to him.

We are given an illustration of the Hindu concept of divine descent in the *Bhagavad-Gita*. The scriptures open with Arjuna, the hero of the *Gita*, seated in a chariot whose driver is Krishna, the divine messenger. They have pulled up on the battlefield to review the opposing armies. The idea of killing his own relatives in battle is shocking to him. He tells Krishna that he cannot take part in such an ignoble affair. This epic then shows how Krishna solved Arjuna's dilemma by a brilliant discourse on the righteousness of war and the duty of a warrior to perceive his rightful role in war. The *Bhagavad-Gita*, however, raises another question in the minds of Christian readers besides that posed by Arjuna. The question concerns itself with the portrayal of Krishna, the divine charioteer, as an *avatar* who has descended of God into man as a manifestation of *Brahman* and the Hindu doctrine of divine descent that is associated with it. For it is here in the *Bhagavad-Gita* that we have one of the clearest expressions of this concept:

> When goodness grows weak,
> When evil increases,
> I make myself a body.
> In every age I come back
> To deliver the holy,
> To destroy the sin of the sinner,
> To establish righteousness.[7]

These lines are spoken by Krishna who has come to earth to stand beside Arjuna in his hour of need. Here is reflected the Hindu belief that God incarnates himself as man from time to time, as he is needed upon earth. There may be many such missions of divine mercy, many such special divine descents whenever, in fact, evil appears on the increase. God coming into human form thus greatly helps the spiritual progress of mankind. As a powerful steamer moves swiftly over the waters, towing rafts and barges in its wake, so when a savior comes "innumerable are the men who find salvation by taking refuge in him." Krishna, of course, is only one of the many prominent saviors or "descents" mentioned in the Hindu scriptures.

Here, again, the Christian is offered an invitation to learn. The classic Christian confession that in Jesus Christ God took on human flesh and dwelt among man is also claimed in some sense in Hinduism, so that this confession is not uniquely Christian. The question is not whether there are such incarnations in Hindu religious thought, but how we are to interpret them and what we are to do with them in the light of Christian doctrine.

Because the divine in Hinduism is a part of, if not actually identical with, all things and beings in the

---

[7] *Bhagavad-Gita,* translated by Christopher Isherwood and Swami Prabhavananda (New York: A Mentor Book, 1954), IV, p. 50.

universe, incarnations can occur in Hinduism with comparative ease. The *avatar* appears without any great cost to God. The *avatar's* life is not of great consequence; in fact, Krishna or Rama or any other manifestation of *Brahman* cannot be said to have performed a single deed or participated in a single event which really makes any difference in the life of anyone living today. The character and life of Krishna, for example, do not add anything to a Hindu's concept of God which he could not learn from other Hindu sources. Krishna's historical existence serves simply to call to mind the great truths that had already been discovered in past ages. For this reason, a Hindu can say without a sense of contradiction that it makes no difference whether Krishna lived at all—the truths were there before Krishna appeared. If this is true of Krishna, the Hindu supposes that this must be true of Christ's life also.

For the Christian, the Gospel is rooted in event and not idea. Not only Jesus' teachings are important to the Christian believer, but also how he lived and died and rose again. Jesus did not come to confirm what was already known of God, but he came to give men a *new* knowledge of God. In this respect one does not talk about religious "ideas" or about the "truths" of religion, but about a historical person and an event rooted in history. When Jesus stated that he was "the truth," he was not speaking of the truth of much learning, or of detached "scientific" discovery, or of "once-for-all" ideas about religion and the universe. The truth which he came to give was set forth in his life. The proper response to his life is not belief or understanding so much as surrender and commitment. The Christian surrenders his life to Christ, for he has seen him as the truth of God, and he is stimulated to a greater personal faith through considering what was really intended when the historical Jesus was named the Christ, the Son of God.

Impact of the Religions

Encounters with other religions are being forced upon us whether we wish it or not or whether we are ready for it or not. In the past there has been reluctance on the part of the whole Christian community to be concerned with the world-wide implications inherent in the Gospel. Most of the missionary impulse, for example, has always come from a "few and special friends of missions," with the result that today there are few Western Christians who have any inkling of what is involved in the impact of the religions. Few Christians are aware of the resurgence of religion in Asia and Africa today. They may be familiar with the political and economic implications as one nation after another finds its identity, but they may fail to see that along with this political and economic activity, the religious history of mankind is taking a monumental turn.

The upsurge of Buddhism and Hinduism, the revived missionary thrust of Islam, especially in Africa, and the proliferation of the sects and the new religions, indicate a new phase in the history of religion. What is taking place affects not only the particular traditions but the whole complex of the religions of man, of which Christianity is a part. As matters stand now, the Christian movement finds itself in profound and fundamental crisis. Some Christians are reluctant to recognize this; almost all fail to see how serious and far-reaching it really is. This is a crisis that reaches every level of the Christian enterprise, the practical as well as the theoretical. So far as our traditional missionary practice and policy is concerned, Max Warren, the Christian missioner, sums up the situation in a three-sentence obituary: "We have marched around alien Jerichos the requisite number of times. We have sounded the trumpets. And the walls have not collapsed." [8] Warren is not exaggerating the crisis. He is simply drawing attention to the seriousness of the new challenge which, many are predicting, will make the impact of science of the past century "turn out to have been as child's play compared with the challenge to Christian theology of the faith of other men." [9] Signs of this challenge are already being observed in the West.

Many students of the religions were pleased with the three-month trip that Paul Tillich took to East Asia where he observed at first hand the faiths of other men. Out of this encounter came his book *Christianity and the Encounter of the World Religions.* Before this trip, it is interesting to note as Wilfred C. Smith has done, that an undergraduate's letter in the *Harvard Crimson,* the student newspaper of the Harvard community, showed that even Tillich's understanding of the religious traditions of the East was not altogether accurate. The point is that it is no longer surprising today to find laymen more conversant with the religions than their pastors, nor is it surprising to find that an undergraduate knows more about the religious traditions of the East than a teacher of Western philosophy and theology. The time is coming, however, when teachers and

[8] Wilfred C. Smith, *The Faith of Other Men* (New York: New American Library, 1963), p. 120.
[9] *Ibid.,* p. 121.

preachers will have to understand the traditions of other religious communities before they will be able to speak for their own. This raises an important issue.

Looking at the matter historically, one may perhaps put it thus: probably Tillich belongs to the last generation of theologians who can formulate their conceptual system as religiously isolationist. The era of religious isolationism is about to be as much at an end as that of political isolationism already is. The pith of Tillich's exposition has to do with this deliberate aptness to the intellectual context in which it appears: the correlation technique, of question and answer. But that context as he sees it is the mental climate of the Western world; and he has spoken to it just at the end of its separatist tradition, just before it is superseded by a new context, a climate modified radically by new breezes, or new storms, blowing in from other parts of the planet. *The new generation of the Church, unless it is content with a ghetto, will live in a cosmopolitan environment, which will make the work of even a Tillich appear parochial.*[10]

Christians and the World Community

For 1,900 years Christian thought has been written within the framework of Greek philosophy, and every writer today is aware that he will be read in the light of it. Since the rise of modern science, Christian sermons have been preached, Christian doctrine has been systematized, and the Christian faith has been expressed within the context of science. No one who wishes a hearing can be unaware of how science has altered our understanding of the faith.

---

[10] *Ibid.*, pp. 121, 122. (Italics are mine.)

Now we stand on the threshold of a new door with regard to the religious traditions of mankind. On this door is written: *Let him who speaks, speak in thought forms and images and contexts that all men in varying religious traditions will understand.* The time must come when a theologian who attempts to work out his own theological position must do so as a member of world community. Within this world society will be found other theologians who are "equally intelligent, equally devout, equally moral," but who are Hindus, Buddhists, and Muslims. The readers of the Christian's theological tracts may be Buddhists, for instance, or if they are not members of another faith, they may have Hindu wives or Muslim colleagues or Zen friends. It will be just as inconceivable for a theologian to construct his system without the worldwide community in mind as it would be for him "to construct an intellectual position unaware that Aristotle has thought about the world or that existentialists have raised new orientations, or unaware that the earth is a minor planet in a galaxy that is vast only by terrestrial standards. Philosophy and science have impinged so far on theological thought more effectively than has comparative religion, but this will not last." [11] While philosophy and science have influenced theological thought more deeply and effectively than have the religions, this situation will soon be altered because of the religious encounter taking place in our one world.

No one knows what new insights will come from the churches in the new situation. The first step, in any case, is to be aware of the coming change. The

---

[11] *Ibid.*, p. 123.

second step is for every Christian to become a part of the worldwide movement of understanding that will hopefully evolve a theology that more nearly reflects the world in which he lives and will set forth with greater meaning and urgency the God who brings light and meaning to it.

Discussion Questions

1. What right does the Christian have to seek the conversion of a Hindu, a Buddhist, or a Muslim?

2. All men—yellow, brown, black, white—are being drawn together. Men are asking: To whom or to what can we turn as a center for this new life? What is the Hindu, Buddhist, and Muslim answer to this question?

3. Until now the Gospel has been viewed in the light of Greek-Roman culture. Was it meant, also, to be viewed in terms of Hindu, Buddhist, and Islamic culture?

4. Which more nearly approximates the biblical approach to the religions? An attitude of:
   a. aggressive condemnation and religious exclusiveness
   b. sympathetic appreciation and cooperation
   c. proclamation of a unique and final Gospel, without denial of other religions

5. Wherein does the Gospel's distinctive and unique claim lie?

6. The church is on the defensive in today's world, as Christendom crumbles and the percentage of Christians in the world becomes smaller. Were Christians ever meant to be massive forces in society, or was the faith meant to be a leaven?

7. In the mission field people talk to those of other faiths about human existence. Does not every man have a right to hear what every fellow human being believes to be the way of salvation from emptiness and meaninglessness?

8. The outreach of the early church resulted from the personal impact of Jesus upon the lives of men and women. It was their response to something which he did for them. Is this what is meant when the Gospel is called "autobiographical"?

9. How much truth can a man grasp directly? How much truth can he stand?

10. Christians come together for worship in order to go apart. That is why the celebration of Holy Communion is an echo of the missionary command contained in Matthew, Chapter 28; it establishes the church in its "layman's" role in the world. Are the present forms of Christian worship adapted with a view to preparing the congregation for service in the world? Or do they turn the worshiper away from his work in the world and make him incapable of performing it?

11. Why is the boundary line between "home" and "foreign," "Christian" and "non-Christian" in missionary thinking no longer valid today? In speaking of the mission of the church, would it be better to make the distinction between church and world everywhere?

12. What does the Christian mean in speaking of eschatological hope in the light of the adherents of other religions when he says: "My faith is particular; my hope is universal"?

13. The Hindu is offended by the Christian's insistence that, in the "once-for-allness" of Christ, he knows all he needs to know about God and salvation. The Hindu asks, "How can you be sure there will not be other Christs who will come and reveal further truth?"

14. Adherents of other religions often suspect that the Christian church relates itself to other faiths to grow stronger at their expense. Is this one of the reasons men are not inclined to listen to its witness?

15. What is meant when it is said that Christianity, at its best, does not claim to be *itself* final and ultimate, but it does seek to witness to that which is final and ultimate, namely to Christ as Lord?

Glossary

Agni	A Vedic god often addressed in the Rig-Veda; a god of fire.
Anatta	Absence of a permanent unchanging self or soul; substanceless.
Anicca	Impermanence; all things are in a state of change.
Arhat	One who is free from all craving and has attained Enlightenment.
Atman	The self; the soul.
Bhagavad-Gita	Most popular of India's scriptures that deals with the discourse between Krishna and Arjuna on the battlefield.
Bhakti-yoga	The path of love; one of the four types of spiritual discipline leading to union with God.
Bodhi Tree	The tree under which Gautama sat during his Enlightenment and named bod-hi, meaning "enlightened" or "wisdom."
Bodhisattva	One destined for Enlightenment: in Mahayana Buddhism, instead of slipping into Nirvana, the Bodhisattva vows to save all beings.
Brahman	Literally, "The Great One," the impersonal God, the Absolute Reality.
Brahman-Atman	Union of Absolute Reality (Brahman) with the True Self (Atman).

127

Buddha	The Enlightened One. There have been many Buddhas in the past and there will be more in the future, Buddhism teaches. The last of the past Buddhas was Siddhartha Gautama. Siddhartha was his personal name, Gautama his family name. He was a member of the Sakya clan.
Confucianism	The ethics of Confucius and his disciples. Filial piety, benevolence, justice, propriety, intelligence, and fidelity are regarded as cardinal virtues.
Dharma	Truth or law; the principle of righteousness; the consequence of action, of Karma; the doctrine of the Buddha.
Dukkha	Misery, suffering, sorrow; the true nature of existence.
Enlightenment	Union with God; Nirvana.
Garuda	The vehicle of Vishnu, also known as Suparna, the Vedic sunbird.
Guru	Spiritual guide or teacher.
Hajj	Pilgrimage to Mecca; the fifth of the Five Pillars of Islam.
Hijrah	Sometimes called Hegira; the migration of Muhammad from Mecca to Medina in 622 A.D.
Hinayana	A term meaning "Little Vehicle," applied to the more conservative Theravada Buddhism.
Incarnations	"Divine descent"—or the descent of God into man.
Indra	The most prominent god in the hymns of the Rig-Veda, the god of the heavens, but later superseded by Vishnu and Shiva.

Islam	Surrender to the divine will as revealed by the prophets of God and, as Muslims believe, the last of the prophets, Muhammad.
Jinn	Demonic group of demi-gods who were worshiped and appeased in Arabia at the time of Muhammad.
Jnana-yoga	The path of knowledge; one of the four fundamental types of spiritual discipline.
Kaaba	The shrine at the center of the great mosque in Mecca and the goal of the Muslim pilgrimage.
Kali at Kalighat	The name of God as the Divine Mother in a particular form in Hinduism.
Karma	Action, deed, work, duty; the law of causation applied in the moral realm, showing that all actions have inevitable moral consequences in this world or the next
Karma-yoga	The path of action; one of the four fundamental paths of spiritual discipline.
Karuna	Compassion, mercy.
Krishna	An incarnation of God, in this case the god Vishnu (the Preserver); God in a general sense.
Mahayana	Literally "the great Vehicle," the Buddhism of China, Tibet, and Japan; it believes that doctrine must grow and change as historical circumstances change.
Maya	The mysterious divine power of Becoming through which God projects the illusory appearance of the cosmos.
Minaret	A slender, lofty tower attached to a mosque and surrounded by one or more balconies from which the summons to prayer is cried by the muezzim.

Mitra	Another Vedic god addressed in the Rig-Veda, a god with some solar characteristics (light), but mainly concerned with vows and compacts.
Mosque	"To bow down or adore"; an Islamic place of public worship.
Muezzin	He who gives the call to prayer from the minaret.
Mukti	Liberation, absolute freedom—the goal of spiritual endeavor
Muslim	He who does "islam," who confesses and witnesses to the Islamic faith and fulfills its duties.
Nirvana	Cessation from all desires which frees a man of the bonds of finite existence; Enlightenment; freedom from the delusions of ego.
Rama	Another incarnation of God, again of the god Vishnu (the Preserver); used also as God in a general sense.
Ramadan	The ninth month of the Muslim year, the month set aside for the annual fast.
Raja-yoga	The path of concentration; one of the four fundamental types of spiritual discipline.
Rig-Veda	Basic hymns, mantras of the Vedas. The Vedas are the primary scriptures of Hinduism.
Salat	"The bowing or kneeling"; the five daily services of worship required of Muslims; the second of the Five Pillars of Islam.
Samadhi	Concentration par excellence, a trance or superconscious state.
Samsara	Life through repeated births and deaths; the worldly life

Sangha	Order of Buddhist monks founded by the Buddha and continued in Theravada Buddhism.
Shinto	Native or indigenous religion of Japan.
Shirk	Act of attributing to other than God the sovereignty and power which properly belongs to God alone.
Skandas	The five "skeins" or aggregates in Buddhism which make up the individual— body, feelings, conceptual knowledge, instincts, and consciousness.
Supreme Ground or Realization	The Absolute *Brahman* of Hinduism. Other words used to designate Brahman are Supreme Spirit, Divine Ground, One Reality, Being Itself, Impersonal Absolute.
Sutras	Aphorism; a terse saying, almost a suggestive formula, embodying a lesson. Different subjects were expressed by Hindu and Buddhist writers through such pithy passages and often taken as authoritative scripture.
Swami	An initiated member of a religious order; one who has renounced the world.
Tanha	Craving, desire; attachment to worldly things.
Taoism	A religion and philosophy of China, traditionally founded by Lao-Tzu, sixth century B.C., and teaching conformity to the cosmic order and simplicity of social and political organization.
Theravada	The Way of the Elders; based on the teachings and practices of the Buddha and found chiefly in Southeast Asia.
Upanishads	Well-known Hindu scriptures included in the Vedas and dwelling mainly upon the eternal truths of life.

Varuna	A Vedic god in the hymns of the Rig-Veda, god of the sea, of the waters.
Vedanta	Literally, "the end of the Vedas."
Vishnu	God as the Preserver, one of the Hindu Trinity (Rama and Krishna are regarded as incarnations of Vishnu).
Yoga	Literally, "union"; union with God and, therefore, any course of spiritual discipline that makes for such union.
Yogi	One who strives for union with God; an aspirant going through any course of spiritual discipline.
Zakat	Almsgiving, as required in Islam; the third of the Five Pillars of Islam.
Zen	The meditative sect of Buddhism in Japan, derived from Ch'an in China.

Index

133